PLAY NICE
IN YOUR
SANDBOX AT
HOME

*How to Enjoy
Peaceful Relationships with the
Most Important People
in Your Life*

Praise for *PLAY NICE in Your Sandbox*

Ron Price is a sage. The wisdom and insight found in *PLAY NICE in Your Sandbox at Home* is timely and delivered in Ron's gentle yet direct manner. He has broken the book into bite-size pieces that are easy to digest. First, his PLAY NICE acronym seamlessly takes us through the marital relationship. His input on common threats hits the nail on the head of the biggest challenges in marriage, and finally, he doesn't just identify potential land mines in marriage; he gives helpful solutions that are practical and easy to apply. Perhaps the best parts of the book are Ron's Chapter Challenges. Honestly, discussing the Chapter Challenges alone will radically change your marriage. I highly recommend Ron Price's *PLAY NICE in Your Sandbox at Home*.

Jay & Laura Laffoon,
Co-founders of Celebrate Ministries, Inc.,
Authors of *He Said She Said*, *The Spark*, and *Make Love Everyday*

Ron Price's *PLAY NICE in Your Sandbox at Home* is packed with practical suggestions and refreshing perspectives anyone can use to begin improving their marriage today. Ron helps you put the past in the proper perspective, enjoy the present, no matter how hectic it may seem, and build a plan for your future that promotes a long, happy marriage.

Nick Pavlidis,
Author of *Confessions of a Terrible Husband:*
Lessons Learned from a Lumpy Couch

PLAY NICE in Your Sandbox at Home is both practical and fun to read. Ron's folksy style and short chapters make it easy to grasp the important principles he wants you to recognize and a challenge at the end of each chapter helps you implement them. He has gathered the best advice from numerous experts in each area, and you will gain valuable insights into your own personal "sandbox" and how to play nice with all those who are important to you now and in the future.

Claudia & David Arp, MSW,
Authors of the *10 Great Dates* series

PLAY NICE in Your Sandbox at Home is a must-read for every marriage, engaged couple, and those seeking to further understand the dynamics of a relationship. The approach of this book delivers a true and practical sense that we all need to refocus and strengthen relationships. We love the way the book brings about a fun and humorous read accompanied with the realism of life that truly will engage any reader.

Kim and Krickitt Carpenter,
#1 *New York Times* Bestselling Authors of *The Vow*

I have known Ron for many years and have had the privilege to interact with him on many occasions. I have always known him to be sincere, intellectually engaging, and thoughtful. This book presents him and his abilities in a quite characteristic way. His book, like Ron himself, speaks with wisdom, humor, and practical applications that will both enlighten and encourage any reader. *PLAY NICE in Your Sandbox at Home* will entertain you as you read it, but much more than that, it will give you information and tools that will truly heal your soul and mend the soul of your relationships. As a committed soul healer myself, I highly recommend this book to you as a way to achieve real intimacy and depth in any relationship you may be a part of.

Dr. Tom Rodgers,
Co-founder with Dr. Beverly Rodgers of Soul Healing Love,
Co-authors of *Adult Children of Divorced Parents*,
and *Becoming a Family that Heals*

Ron is a real hero. He understands that marriage is the basic foundation of civilization, and strong marriages make for safer, more productive, and kinder societies. Beyond that, he knows that marriage is hard and many people are ill-equipped to handle the troubles they find. In our current society, which holds little value for marriage, he stands out as one of the heroes who is willing to help couples find a path to keeping their marriage strong. This fantastic book is fun to read, enlightening, and truly helpful.

Bill Sharer,
New Mexico State Senator

Easy to read, insightful, relevant, and practical, *PLAY NICE in Your Sandbox at Home* is a wonderful offering to couples, whether dating or married. It provides relationship insights and principles and most important, relationship skills that allow a couple to take a good relationship to a great one, a hurting relationship to a healing relationship. Being in the marriage and family therapy community for over 25 years, *PLAY NICE in Your Sandbox at Home* will be a book I strongly encourage couples to put into practice.

Richard Marks, Ph.D.,
Executive Director, Marriage for Life, Inc.

PLAY NICE
IN YOUR
SANDBOX AT
HOME

*How to Enjoy
Peaceful Relationships with the
Most Important People
in Your Life*

By Ron Price, MA

PlayNiceInYourSandbox.com

ron@PlayNiceInYourSandbox.com

Published by Productive Outcomes, Inc.
1909 E. 20th Street
Farmington, NM 87401

ISBN-13: 978-0-9980644-2-0
ISBN-10: 0-9980644-2-4

Edited by Jennifer Harshman of HarshmanServices.com
Cover Design by Sam Perera of BrandsBySam.com
Book Design and Formatting by James Woosley of FreeAgentPress.com

For general information on our other products and services, please go to PlayNiceInYourSandbox.com or mailto:ron@PlayNiceinYourSandbox.com.

Please refer others there so they can get this book for themselves.

I am pleased to dedicate this book to my loving wife, Maridell, who has put up with me through thick and thin and helped me learn much about resolving conflicts in the home.

Contents

THE PLAY NICE MODEL:

FOREWORD

THE HISTORY OF OUR world has been written by unsung heroes. Men and women who are largely unrecognized, unknown, and indisputably valuable. Look at the genealogy of Jesus and ask how many names you recognize. Stroll through Arlington National Cemetery and ask how many of these soldiers' stories you are aware of. Look over the list of teachers at your favorite educational institution and ask how much you know about any of them. We know little about them, but our lives are not possible without them.

In my opinion, Ron Price is one of these unsung heroes. He is well-read, well-educated and well-connected. He is uniquely committed to discovering how relationships work and how to make that knowledge accessible to average people. He is well-versed in relationship theory but speaks the language of everyday. He understands the principles that make relationships thrive and is committed to translating these truths into simple, practical steps ordinary people can put into action.

In *PLAY NICE in Your Sandbox at Home*, Ron presents some of the best relationship information available today. He does so as a traveler rather than a reporter. He has been in the trenches with couples who are trying to figure out how to stay in love, resolve conflict, overcome disappointment, and keep their rhythm as a couple amidst the rigors of family responsibility. He speaks from his decades of intense experience as a divorce mediator. He shares from the hundreds of presentations he has attended. He reveals what he has absorbed from some of the best thinkers of our day.

PLAY NICE in Your Sandbox at Home is more of a handbook than a novel. Ron presents proven skills in bite-sized pieces so you can find practical steps that will enhance your relationships by reading just a few pages at a time. Of course, you can read the entire work in a few sittings, but I think you will find that you will need to stop reading on a regular basis so you can practice being in love rather than just read about being in love.

I first met Ron when my wife, Pam, and I spoke for the marriage event he hosts annually in Farmington, NM. I found Ron to be genuine, sincere, and naturally humorous. I also found him to be passionate about marriage and family relationships and deeply committed to helping others succeed at these heart-felt connections.

Joseph Campbell writes, "A hero is someone who has given his or her life to something bigger than oneself."[1] If this is the case, Ron Price is a modern-day, little-known hero who is making a real difference in people's vital relationship.

I hope you learn to *PLAY NICE in Your Sandbox at Home* as you take this practical journey with my friend Ron.

Sincerely,

Bill Farrel
Author of *Men Are Like Waffles, Women Are Like Spaghetti* and *The 10 Best Decisions a Man Can Make*

---

1   https://www.brainyquote.com/quotes/quotes/j/
josephcamp138795.html?src=t_hero

PREFACE

THERE ARE TIMES I wonder what makes me think I should write a book on marriage advice when there are so many others far more qualified than I am who have already done so. Marriage advice and wisdom abounds in our society, and I recently rediscovered some which I had learned long ago. Though I don't know the last names of these "experts," I do know and will share with you their first names and ages.

Marlon, age 10, tells us that at the wedding "a man and a woman promise to go through sickness and illness and diseases together." I guess he's right, but it's not the cheeriest thought I've had all day.

If you've ever wondered, "What is the best age to marry?" your answer may come from Cam, who at age 10 says, "Twenty-three is the best age, because you know the person FOREVER by then!"

And, lastly, Allan, age 10, has some advice for men on how to select a wife. He states, "You got to find somebody who likes the same stuff. Like if you like sports, she should like it that you like sports, and she should keep the chips and dip coming."

Okay, maybe I get to keep writing—at least for a little while. Actually, what I feel best qualifies me to be a marriage "expert" is that I attended nine Smart Marriage Conferences and attended well over 100 workshops and plenary speeches given by experts who have devoted their lives to help people understand and succeed in marriage.

Each Smart Marriage Conference featured numerous keynote, banquet, and plenary speakers along with some 90–160 workshops on various marriage skills. There were also several one, two, or three-day training institutes held both before and after the three-day conferences.

At my first conference in 2001, I attended a three-day pre-conference institute and got certified to lead PREP, the Prevention and Relationship Enhancement Program. PREP now stands for Prevention and Relationship Education Program, and to say this program has had a profound impact on me would be a gross understatement. Its influence will become obvious as I cite their research numerous times in this book.

I led my first PREP class in 2002, and realized I truly enjoyed helping people succeed in marriage. In 2003, I co-founded a non-profit organization, now known as The Four Corners Coalition for Marriage & Family, for which

I still serve as Executive Director. From 2011 until 2017, I wrote a weekly column in the Farmington (NM) Daily Times, in which I addressed marriage enhancement matters.

I published my first book, *PLAY NICE in Your Sandbox at Work*, in October 2016, where I provide a model to prevent conflict (PLAY) and resolve conflict (NICE), whichever is most appropriate. I then give numerous tips and techniques to help people deal with conflict productively in the workplace.

Here's how I explained the Sandbox connection in the introduction to that book:

> *"The concept of a sandbox brings back fond memories of peaceful times without a care in the world. The sandbox experience is, in many ways, a great analogy for life.*
>
> *In the sandbox experience of our youth, we learned several lessons that guide us in our present day-to-day existence. We learned to work with others in building projects. We learned how to resolve differences of opinion. We learned that we were expected to play nicely with others—thus the origin of the phrase "play nice in the sandbox." Most of us would agree that this is sometimes more easily said than done."*

I think you'll agree the Sandbox analogy holds as true for home situations as it does for those we face at work.

This book follows a similar pattern to the original. While not as specific to preventing or resolving conflict, the PLAY NICE model does provide helpful practices to do just that. In each section, I provide helpful principles that contribute to a lasting, satisfying marriage. We'll also look at some common threats to marital bliss and satisfaction, and some helpful pointers to prevent them from stealing your joy. There are reasons why people who blissfully say "I do!" move fairly quickly to "No, I don't!" We'll address several of those underlying reasons and provide you with solutions so it does not have to happen to you.

While I'm confident you will find helpful information in this book, you will also notice I cite numerous other resources throughout. I interviewed Dr. Greg Smalley, the head of the counseling department at Focus on the Family, and son of the late Dr. Gary Smalley. He told me that he and his wife choose a marriage enrichment book to read together during the Christmas season each year. To be honest, I was taken back by his statement. Here is a man who quite possibly knows more about marriage and family wellness than anyone on the planet, yet he takes the time to continue learning and growing. I feel safe in saying if he feels the need, it likely makes great sense for the rest of us.

Marriage is serious business, and with the proper knowledge and skills, most couples could do life quite well together. That is certainly my hope for you. If you enjoy reading this book, I strongly encourage you to purchase a copy of *PLAY NICE in Your Sandbox at Work*. All of the tips and techniques you'll find there will have direct application to your home as well as your work.

ACKNOWLEDGMENTS

I especially want to thank the following people who contributed mightily to this endeavor:

Although this book is not intended solely for a Christian audience, I do want to acknowledge my gratitude to my Lord and Savior Jesus Christ, Who entrusted me to share the information contained herein.

I am pleased and honored to call Bill Farrel my friend. I don't know how to adequately express how much I value the numerous, highly constructive contributions he made to this book. You won't be aware of them, but I promise you will be appreciative.

Keith Barbeau and his fine staff at the Farmington, NM Courtyard by Marriott, where much of this book was written.

Donele Fowler, Fred Henry and the fine staff at the Farmington, NM Best Western Plus where it was completed.

Diane Sollee and the far-too-many-to-list contributors to the Smart Marriage Conferences I was privileged to attend. Many of the people I met there became guest writers for my newspaper column and radio guests on my radio program TWOgether as ONE.

Jennifer Harshman and James Woosley for taking my words and making them so much better, and so much more pleasant to read.

Bill Sharer for his resolute defense of marriage and family in the NM State Legislature.

The staff and management at the Farmington, NM Daily Times—past and present—who enabled me to write my weekly column for 5+ years: John Elchert, Troy Turner, Sammy Lopez, Chris Roberts, Maggie Wegrzyn, Hannah Grover, and Jennifer Knight. I am truly grateful for all those who told me often they read and appreciated the column.

Carl Brenner, my co-founder of the Four Corners Coalition for Marriage & Family and all the board members—past and present: Randy Joslin, Dr. Mike Hattabaugh, Msgr. Leo Gomez, Darrel & Christie Clark, Wilann Thomas, Lee Fiske, Jay & Gloria Wendeborn, Steve & Martha Thomas, Jason & Rebekah Oberholser, Ryan & Krista Johnson, Mike Justice, and Gene Chapin.

Many others who have had a profound influence on me are cited throughout the book or listed in the resource section at the back. I encourage you to check out some of them for further help in making or keeping your marriage great.

NOTE TO READER

Throughout this book you will find several Quick Response (QR) Codes and internet links which are tied to brief interviews with guest experts. To access these videos, download a free QR Code Reader from your App Store. Once activated simply hold the scanner over the Code and the video should pop up. You can also type the link into your browser and view it that way as well.

**ProductiveOutcomes.com/
brief-intro**

Nothing is perfect. Life is messy. Relationships are complex. Outcomes are uncertain. People are irrational.

–Hugh Mackay

INTRODUCTION

I HEARD A PARABLE ABOUT a man who died and went to Heaven. Immediately upon his entrance, he was fitted with a three-foot-long fork surgically attached to his right hand and a three-foot-long spoon surgically attached to his left hand. He thought this was rather odd, but since he was where he wanted to be and since all the others were similarly configured, he did not mind.

The next thing he noticed was that there was food everywhere he looked. Table after table after table of enticing food that smelled wonderful and looked fantastic.

His final observation was that the people seemed to be truly happy and congenial. They were all smiling and seemed to be so kind and gentle with each other. He was certain he was going to enjoy his new home. He had just one question to ask his attending angel. He had always heard so much about Hell and he wondered if he could be permitted a quick peek just to satisfy his curiosity.

The angel informed him that there were daily tours of Hell at 2:00 p.m. HST (Heaven Standard Time) and that he should be by the elevator to take the tour. At 2:00 p.m., he stood at the elevator with several other new residents. The doors opened they got in and down they went. I mean down, down, down—okay, you get the picture—down they went.

After a time, the elevator stopped, the doors opened, and he and the others were looking at Hell. The first thing he noticed was that everyone in Hell had a three-foot-long fork surgically attached to their right hand and a three-foot-long spoon surgically attached to their left hand.

Next he noticed that there was food everywhere he looked. Table after table after table of what looked and smelled like great food, but he wasn't going to get off the elevator for a closer inspection.

His final observation was that the people seemed to be miserable. They were yelling at each other, hitting each other, and just totally discontented with their situation.

The tour concluded, the elevator doors closed and he began his ascent back to Heaven. En route, he was totally perplexed. All residents of both Heaven and Hell had the same forks and spoons, and apparently the same array of fine dining, yet in Heaven they could not be happier and in Hell they could not be more miserable.

It wasn't until he got back to Heaven that he realized the difference. You see, in Heaven, the people were using their utensils to serve one another, while in Hell they were trying to serve themselves and it just could not be done.

I have often shared this illustration with my marriage coaching clients as I believe it is a wonderful analogy of what marriage should be. Rather than each spouse seeking their own gratification, he and she should focus more on how to meet their mate's needs and desires. As with any illustration, you should not take this too far. I am not at all suggesting that you pay no attention to your own needs, but merely that your mate's needs occupy much of your time and consideration.

As you are about to read, successful marriage does not typically happen without some specific elements in place. It always amazes me when couples come to me for help with their marriage that they seem surprised to be in that situation. Far too many couples have a false image of marriage—either that it will be a grin-and-bear-it ordeal, or it will be nonstop bliss and contentment. Each of these extremes misses the mark.

The PLAY NICE model for marriage is certainly not perfect nor all-inclusive, but put into practice, it will give you a solid footing from which to venture into life, as I like to say, TWOgether as ONE.

When you look at your life, the greatest happinesses are family happinesses.

—Dr. Joyce Brothers

SECTION ONE
PLAY NICE

Play Together, Stay Together.

YOU MIGHT REMEMBER THE saying "The family that prays together stays together." I'll leave that discussion to the theologians among us. I believe the couple and the family that regularly plays together greatly increases the odds they will stay together.

When couples first meet and begin to get attracted to each other, they do things together. I hope that you can remember the early days of your relationship. Likely you enjoyed going for walks, on picnics, to the movies, dancing, etc. It didn't matter so much what you did as the fact that you did it together.

My guess is you had so much fun together, you eventually decided to do it forever, and you got married. Many couples continue the fun as a regular feature of their marriage long after the honeymoon, but unfortunately, over time, life issues can creep in and crowd out opportunities to have fun. If you're not careful your marriage can center around raising the kids and paying the bills. Or is it raising the bills and paying the kids? Either way, it is a threat to your happiness as a couple.

You simply must make the time to have fun on a regular and recurring basis. Far too many couples have lost the practice of regular dating. Please don't be one of those couples. Set times together just for the two of you. I suggest a minimum of twice each month, but weekly might be an even better idea. These don't have to be expensive or extravagant dates. Just being together in an enjoyable activity and laughing together is a tremendous positive factor in keeping your marriage alive and strong. I've seen research that suggests that simply sitting beside each other enjoying a funny movie or television show can help you feel close and appreciate each other.

Be careful to protect your fun time from conflict. Most of us can recall times when we headed off to dinner or a movie or another enjoyable event only to have an inadvertent conflict arise and spoil the entire evening. Please don't let this happen. Agree together in advance that this time is set aside for fun and that any conflicts which might arise will automatically be postponed to a more appropriate time.

Be creative in trying out new experiences. Sure, you have a favorite place to vacation, but is that really the only enjoyable spot on the planet to reconnect with each other? Of course, you have a favorite restaurant, but is that truly the only place you can find culinary satisfaction and an enjoyable time together?

Set aside some time to brainstorm activities or events you might want to investigate. Geocaching, Frisbee golf, bowling, or a pottery or massage class at your local community college are just a few quick ideas that popped into my head that you likely have not engaged in recently—if ever. How about setting aside time to bake cookies together or to do playful battle with laser tag or paintball?

Again, the "what" part of what you do is secondary to the actual "doing" of maintaining fun in your marriage. It is vital to the overall health and wellness of your relationship.

So here are two suggestions to help you play together regularly. The first comes from my PREP training and is called the Deck of Ten. To start, each of you needs to have ten index cards. On each index card, write down one thing you would like to do together just for fun and just the two of you. Some of these cards should list simple, inexpensive, easy-to-do activities like going for a walk or a bike ride or having a picnic. Some of the cards could be more complex such as taking a cruise or going to Disneyworld.

Once each spouse has compiled their deck of cards, begin the alternating process of drawing a card from your mate's deck. It is then your privilege to make sure whatever is listed on the card takes place. For instance, if your spouse wrote down "I want us to go to dinner and a movie," you then take the initiative to make the necessary arrangements.

Again, some of the cards will be doable quickly and easily while some may require extensive planning. If you draw one of the latter cards, break the process into smaller steps such as doing research online to find what options might be available, costs involved, best times of the year, etc. Schedule a time to continue the planning process and then draw another card for more immediate implementation. You might also consider having each of your children have their own deck of ten for activities to do as a family.

For the second tip, you'll need to visit the website marriagebuilders.com. This is the website for Dr. Willard Harley, author of (among many other books) *His Needs, Her Needs*, a mega-bestseller on how to do marriage well. Once at the site, do a search for his Recreational Enjoyment Inventory. Print out a copy for each of you and begin to fill it in individually. After you have each completed the inventory, combine your answers to discover activities you both would enjoy doing together.

I know many parents feel guilty going out on a date or being away from their children. This guilt is often exasperated by the displeasure shown by the child as you head out the door. Yes, it can be hard to leave a crying child with a trusted babysitter—but do it anyway. Notice I said "trusted" babysitter. He or she will likely soon be able to get your child engaged in some fun activity of their own, thereby replacing their feelings of abandonment with hope that you don't come home too soon. You might also consider childcare sharing with another couple who can watch your children while you go out, and then you can return the favor for their date night.

During my 29-year career as a divorce mediator, I met numerous couples who told me they decided to put the children first and focused on them more than on their marriage. Big mistake! If you truly want to put your children first, focus on your marriage and give them what they actually want and need most of all—two parents who love each other and are together for them.

I like the analogy of the flight attendant's instructions on what to do if the air mask drops down while you are traveling with small children. They tell you to put the mask on yourself first and then to assist your children. Isn't that being selfish and unloving? Not at all! The theory is that if you are incapacitated, you will be of no help to your children. So make sure you're okay first, and then help them. The same can be said about your marriage. Give it the time and attention it deserves, and you will be in a far better position to help your children.

Michelle Weiner-Davis bills herself as a "guerilla divorce buster." Her book *Divorce Busting* has helped numerous couples reclaim the joy they once shared and the hope they initially held for a happy life together. In her book, couples learn these skills and more:

- ways to leave the past behind and set attainable goals
- strategies for identifying problem-solving behavior that works—and how to make changes last
- "uncommon-sense" methods for breaking unproductive patterns

Perhaps chief among the skills she teaches couples is the importance of having fun like they used to. Remember the little tokens of affection you gave to each other in those early days of your relationship—the silly cards or notes, the innocent pranks you played on each other, the time you took to fully listen to each other and discover each other's personality and character. Especially focus on the fun times you had together going on walks or picnics or to the movies, etc.

Now ask yourself a question: when was the last time you did any of those things?

Mrs. Davis encourages her readers and clients to go back and do the things they did when they first fell in love, and they will likely rediscover their love for, and enjoyment of, each other. That is, I might add, assuming that those activities were legal then and still are now.

I have often recommended this tactic to my clients and am a firm believer that it has great benefit in turning around a marriage which has grown stale. Obviously, some marriages will be in more severe circumstances and will require more intense intervention. But I strongly suggest you try the "have fun together like we used to" approach before you get to that point.

Here's a tip I learned from my friend and colleague Dr. Mike Hattabaugh. Every wedding anniversary is and should be special and deserving of some form of celebration. Dr. Mike recommends that every five years is cause for special celebration. Neither he nor I recommend you break the bank and go into huge debt, but some indulgence is justified.

The beauty behind this every-five-year plan is that you spend a couple of years planning and dreaming and saving. Let your imagination and excitement run wild. Use the internet, visit a local travel agent or cruise specialist, talk to friends about wonderful trips they have taken.

You then go on your excursion and have a wonderful time. As travel can often be hectic, you might want to agree in advance that you will not let frustration or upsetting circumstances steal away the joy of your time together. Determine in advance to make delays and unexpected circumstances a part of the adventure.

Upon your return, you have pictures, memories, and stories to enjoy for the next few years. By then it's time to start planning the next one. Let me encourage you to put this plan into practice no matter where you are in your marital journey. For those of you who are newlyweds, I have a lock-tight, money-back guarantee for you. If you follow through with this plan for ten cycles, you will positively reach the 50-year milestone in your marriage. How about that? I'm not only a marriage coach—I'm a mathematician as well!

Am I suggesting that all marital problems can be fixed by having fun together? Absolutely not. Am I suggesting that fun is crucial to maintaining a healthy marriage and to repairing one that is somewhat broken? Absolutely yes! Why not give it a try and find out for yourself?

CHAPTER CHALLENGE

Set aside some time this week to brainstorm with your spouse how you can ensure that having fun will be a major component of your marriage. Consider partnering with some friends who have children near the age of yours and trade off babysitting while the other couple gets some much needed "us" time. Create your Deck of Ten and download and complete the Recreational Enjoyment Inventory. And lastly visit Dr. Hattabaugh's podcast at MikeHattabaugh.com.

DAVE & CLAUDIA ARP

Dave and Claudia Arp are well-known in the field of marriage enrichment. They are the developers of the Ten Great Dates program which has helped untold thousands of couples maintain or reinvigorate their marriage. Please take a few moments to hear their thoughts on the importance of structured dating to the overall health and satisfaction of your marriage.

**ProductiveOutcomes.com/
dave-claudia-arp**

I've stopped trying to get ahead. That way, I can concentrate on trying to slow down the rate at which I am falling behind.

—Source Unknown

CHAPTER P1

Whelmed? Surely You Can do Better—Can't You?

I'M THINKING OF TAKING my life in a new direction with my ultimate goal to be *whelmed*. To be honest, I don't know what whelmed is, but I know I don't want too much or too little of it. In regards to a healthy marriage, being either overwhelmed or underwhelmed can pose serious problems.

The term "overwhelmed" probably doesn't need much elaboration. I believe it is the scourge of our age—or at least one of them. I don't know many people who are not stretched these days in far too many directions.

I called a friend to ask him to get involved in a project I was working on. After hearing the list of tasks he currently had on his plate, I was exhausted. I, of course, graciously withdrew my request.

This friend's story is anything but unique. It is important to realize from time to time that your life may be out-of-control busy, and if that is the case, your marriage is bound to suffer. You simply won't have the time or energy to give it the attention it deserves. I read a book several years ago by Dr. Richard Swenson called *Margin.* This is an excellent resource for getting a grip on over-commitments and on how to build in periods of respite into your busyness. I think I need to carve out some time to read it again.

Along those lines, may I suggest that you take the time to schedule activities and events which are important to the overall health of your marriage. We've all heard the expression "find time" to do something. If you have figured out a way to find time, would you please let me know? I've been looking for time for a long time.

To "take time" or "make time" seems far more realistic than to try to "find time." Among the elements which might be worthy of your time are play times just for fun, the state-of-your-marriage conversations, parenting meetings, and even sex.

What did I just say? That's right, many couples routinely schedule times for physical intimacy. They consider it important enough to make it a priority and something which should not get pushed to the side by other life demands. I've also heard that one gender in particular prefers some advance notice, while one just needs the other to show up. I'll let you guess which gender might be which.

I can't promise that proper scheduling and prioritizing will do away with all overwhelm in your life, but as my Jewish grandmother used to say, "That and some chicken soup couldn't hurt."

Regarding being underwhelmed in your marriage, you simply must take steps to prevent it from happening. I can't tell you how many folks have come to me for marriage help telling me they have drifted apart. What I can tell you is that this is the likely result when couples stop focusing on their marriage and making it a priority in their lives.

There is nothing wrong with each partner having their own personal interests and pursuits in life—so long as these are not a threat to the marriage or causing undue hardship on your mate. But a couple who spend the majority of their time with each doing his or her own thing is likely a couple I will someday see for divorce mediation.

CHAPTER CHALLENGE

Schedule time to discuss where you and your spouse fall on the overwhelmed-underwhelmed continuum. Make a plan to ensure you keep time for fun and other important components of a healthy marriage.

The shortest distance between two people is a story.
—**Patti Digh**

CHAPTER P2
High-Low-Learn

ONE OF MY FAVORITE movies is *The Story of Us*, which stars Bruce Willis and Michelle Pfeiffer. It's a Rob Reiner film, which tells you two things right off. One is that it likely has a family-friendly theme and two, the language is horrible and definitely not family-friendly. If you can get through the language, however, *The Story of Us* has a very powerful message for couples in marriage.

Without giving away too much of the movie, I'll tell you that it details how a very young Bruce and Michelle meet and fall madly in love. Love leads to marriage, marriage leads to children, children and life lead to difficulties, and ultimately difficulties lead to divorce. If that's where the story ended, I likely wouldn't recommend it. But I wish every couple in America—make that the world—could view the final scene. It alone could deter many couples from going through with their divorce and inspire them instead to reenergize their efforts to make their marriage work.

While I'm on the subject of marriage-friendly movies, another personal favorite is *Fireproof*, in which Kirk Cameron wakes up to the fact that he is largely responsible for the impending demise of his marriage. Rather than waste time blaming his likely soon-to-be-ex-wife, he goes on the difficult journey to win back her heart. It's rated PG (Parental Guidance Suggested). I believe the rating is due to the graphic depiction of Christianity, and of course we simply must guard our children against such potentially harmful material. But that's a subject for another time.

Both of these movies drive home the point that marriage is supposed to be for keeps. Every married person will encounter difficult times when he or she does not like his or her spouse very much. This is normal and to be expected. If it happens repeatedly, then, by all means, get help. But for those occasional blowups, assuming they are not violent or abusive, the best response is usually to take some time to let things calm down and address them later when cooler heads can prevail. Trust me, you don't want to say things to each other when you are angry or upset. I believe it was George Thompson, author of *Verbal Judo*, who advised: "Never use words that rise readily to your lips, or you'll give the greatest speech you'll ever live to regret."

Now lest you think I'm auditioning to be a movie critic, I guess I should let you know the main point of this chapter.

It's a game I adapted from *The Story of Us,* and one which I wholeheartedly recommend to couples and families. In the movie, the parents asked the children to tell them what was the high point of their day and what was the low point of their day. As memory serves, the parents then also answered the same questions. The game is called High-Low, and it's a good way to find out what's going on in the daily lives of your loved ones.

My adaptation of this game is to add a third component—learn. In High-Low-Learn, you still inquire into the high points and low points, but you also ask, "What did you learn today?" It's a lot better than asking "What did you do in school today?" and hearing the typical "nothing" response. By playing this game on a frequent and regular basis—daily could work well—you will find the family drawing closer together and being more aware of what's going on in each one's life. This is also very helpful way to build or maintain a strong marriage.

According to John Gottman Ph.D., a noted marriage and family researcher and Professor Emeritus of Psychology at the University of Washington, "A powerful predictor of relationship stability is how much detail each partner knows about the other's life." At his website[2], you can download his Love Map Exercise, which is a game designed to "bring partners closer by helping them get more familiar with each other's world. Thoughtful questions and additional opportunity questions enable partners to connect emotionally, and increase intimacy and understanding in a fun, gentle way." You can also purchase his highly regarded book *The Seven Principles for Making Marriage Work,* in which you'll find his 20-question Love Map Game.

---

2   https://www.gottman.com/wp-content/uploads/2016/09/
    Love-Maps-White-Paper.pdf

We tend to invest in things or causes that are important to us. May I suggest you give some thought to investing in your marriage and your family. I am talking about investing some money, but perhaps more importantly, investing your time. I can just about guarantee you a wonderful rate of return on that investment.

CHAPTER CHALLENGE

Take some time to visit gottman.com and see the variety of resources listed there. Download the Love Map or another of the communication resources they have. Then schedule time—perhaps the same time each week—to get to know each other more deeply than you do now. Also, introduce your children to high-low-learn and make it a regular, fun activity for all.

*I believe that
the greatest gift
you can give
your family and
the world is a
healthy you.*

—Joyce Meyer

CHAPTER P3
Here's to Your Health

SOMEWHERE IN MY MATHEMATICS education, I learned a formula that if A=B, and B=C, then A=C. Here's a formula I made up myself: if husband is healthier, and wife is healthier, the chances of the couple having a healthy marriage improve dramatically. It also stands to reason that better health should lead to increased energy and increased energy should lead to more time for fun activities.

To that end, let me give you a helpful way to remember how to take good mental, emotional, physical, and spiritual care of yourself. Some years ago, I came across an acronym for overall health and wellness called NEWSTART. This acronym was developed at Weimar Institute, a Seventh-day Adventist health facility in Weimar, California.

The *N* in NEWSTART stands for "Nutrition," which likely is no surprise. Remember the old expression "You are what you eat?" I'm not sure that is totally true—at least I hope it's not, for the humanitarians I know. Okay, bad joke, but it does make perfect sense that what you put into your body will have a dramatic impact on your overall state of wellness.

The *E* you can likely guess is for "Exercise," which has gotten lots of positive news coverage in recent decades but is still woefully lacking in the lives of many Americans. *W* stands for "Water." Research is abundant and clear that to live healthfully, one must stay adequately hydrated. This means you consume water in its purest form before you get thirsty and stay ahead of your thirst. All year long, but especially when cold-and-flu season approaches, staying well hydrated is one of the best protections you can incorporate into your life.

The *S* in NEWSTART is for "Sunshine." Much has been written in recent years about the health benefits of Vitamin D. Sunshine, with appropriate moderation and sensible protection, of course, is a wonderful source of this important vitamin. *T* is for "Temperance" and serves as a reminder that even good things taken to extremes can have harmful effects.

A reminds us that fresh "air" and proper breathing form a key component of good health. Studies show that many of us do not breathe properly resulting in fatigue and other challenges.

The *R* is for "rest," another element of life that seems to be lacking in so much of our population. We are a sleep-deprived nation, and the effects are widespread and often traumatic. The final *T* is for "Trust in Divine Power."

We are physical, mental, emotional, and spiritual beings, and to avoid paying attention to any of these areas of life is to invite less-than-acceptable levels of overall satisfaction and wellness. Having faith in God and living in that faith has been shown to yield tremendous life benefits.

Each of these elements of good health deserves an entire chapter or two on their own, but that is not my purpose for this book. Abundant information is readily available in your community and online to help you know how to eat well, exercise well, etc. The problem in our society today is not a lack of knowledge as much as it is a lack of execution. I think you would admit that pursuing good physical health is a worthy life goal, but do you spend some time investigating what it takes to live healthfully?

I realize that disease and poor health will occur despite our best efforts and that certainly does not mean the marriage is doomed. But that truth does not take away from the reality that when each partner makes personal health a priority and focus, the marriage will likely reap benefits.

So when was the last time you and your spouse considered how well you are doing health-wise? Are you challenging and encouraging each other to be intentional about how you're feeding your body, your mind, and your spirit? It may not always be easy to make healthy decisions for life, but consider the alternative—it's not a pretty picture.

Along with the normal recommendations for health such as diet, exercise, rest, water, etc., I want to add one more you may not typically consider: laughter. Laughter has many health benefits. In fact, there is an entire science called gelotology which is dedicated to the study of the health benefits of laughter. Laughter can reduce blood pressure by increasing vascular blood flow and oxygenation of the blood. Hearty laughter is a good physical workout as it exercises muscles in the diaphragm, face, legs, and back. The respiratory system also gets worked well during hearty laughter, and stress hormones such as cortisol and adrenaline are reduced. Laughter is said to improve one's immune system and improve alertness, creativity, and memory. Someone remind me please that I may need to laugh more—just in case I forget.

So to do my part in improving your overall health and that of your marriage, allow me to share with you some words of wit I picked up along my life's journey. I heard of a nine-year-old boy named Johnny who was spending a few days visiting his grandmother. He came in from playing one day and asked his grandmother what it's called when two people sleep in the same room and one is on top of the other. Grandmother was a little taken aback, but she decided to tell him the truth. She said, "It's called having sex," to which the boy replied, "Okay, Grandma," and went back out to play.

A short while later Johnny came in, rather irritated, and told grandma, "it is **not** called having sex. It is called 'bunk beds' and Billy's mother wants to speak with you right now!"

George Bernard Shaw said, "You don't stop laughing when you grow old; you grow old when you stop laughing." So if it's been a while since you and your spouse have done some serious laughing together, may I suggest you not waste many more moments before correcting this imbalance.

CHAPTER CHALLENGE

Set a time to evaluate your overall health. Determine to take steps to improve in areas that need improvement and to maintain in areas that are currently working for you. Map out a strategy with specific objectives and timelines for how you are going to take good care of yourself. Be sure to include regular times for fun and laughter in your overall plan.

While you're working on your own health and wellness, it's okay to encourage your spouse to take good care of him or herself as well. If you do suggest that, please do so with a gentle, loving spirit. And only say it when you are committed to doing the same for him or her. Just for fun, you might want to Google the 1929 song "Button Up Your Overcoat." It reinforces the point that I'm making here.

Bettering yourself is a big deal. When you're feeling good, it is easier to put up with little annoyances and not let them get the best of you. When you're feeling good, it is easier for you to give and receive love from your mate than when you're down or discouraged or ailing in some way.

I have never seen a monument erected to a pessimist.

—Paul Harvey

SECTION TWO
PLAY NICE

Look for the Good:
Seek and you will find

PLEASE STOP WHAT YOU'RE doing and get a pen and some paper. Okay, now jot down two or three criticisms of your mate. Just take a moment (by the way, the official definition of a moment is 90 seconds) and list two or three of his or her imperfections. Alright, now that you've done that, take the same pen and paper and write down two or three of your mate's positive qualities. List two or three aspects of him or her which you find noteworthy and commendable.

I'm curious. Which list was easier to compile?

I guess that depends on the overall quality of your marriage. If your marriage is good and you're happy together, the second list was likely the easier, although the first list is always doable. I truly believe developing the habit of looking for and focusing on the good in one's mate can transform a challenged marriage into a successful and healthy one, and keep a good marriage thriving.

It is a psychological principle that what you focus on tends to grow. When you focus on the negative aspects of life, of which we all have at least a few, your thoughts tend to gravitate toward the negative. Focusing on the positive aspects of your life will not make the negative ones disappear, but you will find they have less power to influence your mood and thoughts during your day.

Please know the first mistake you made in getting married was that you married a human being who, by definition, is going to have faults and who is going to do things that annoy you at times. Unless he or she married someone other than a human, you might not want to be too quick to pass judgment.

I appreciate this Zig Ziglar quote: "Some people do really find fault like there's a reward for it." It's so easy to find fault, and so many of us do. What's ironic, however, is that those times when you are most critical are usually the times you're most upset with yourself. Since you've got to live with yourself and your thoughts, you can only take so much self-abuse and criticism. After a time, you will naturally look for another outlet to blame for your state of being upset. All too often, that other outlet is going to be your spouse, or perhaps your children.

That may be a common and normal practice, but it's not right, and it's certainly not conducive to a healthy marriage or family. I watched a video performance by the Peculiar

People drama group called Repentance which makes a great point in a comical way. A husband tells his wife he wants to discuss the sermon they heard in church that morning. The wife agrees, but then he asks her to go first. The message of the sermon was repentance, and he suggested they should start their conversation with her telling him what she needed to repent of.

Needless to say, the conversation did not get off to a good start. The wife got justifiably upset that he would try to railroad her into admitting her faults and she took great offense. They then go on to point out each other's need for repentance and the conversation gets ugly and loud.

Finally, the husband has a change of heart and admits that he wanted to have the conversation so he could repent, but it was difficult for him to do so. He apologizes for starting the conversation by putting pressure on her, and he offers a sincere, heartfelt expression of regret for the way things are going in their marriage. He acknowledges his anger and the destructive impact it has had on her and their children.

The wife's reaction is heartwarming. Rather than continuing to jump his case, she softens and accepts his apology with humility. She then begins to list some of her faults and relates what she has done to steal the joy from their relationship. They stop attacking each other and begin to encourage and lift each other up—which, by the way, is what married folks are supposed to do.

We live in a rude world, and we get used to people putting us down or disappointing us in some way. Home is supposed to be the place where each one is rooted for, valued, supported, and believed in. When you get criticized and put down at home, the pain goes deep, and the resentment even deeper.

So what am I saying? That you should never tell your mate when something he or she is doing is upsetting you? Not a chance. But I'm certain you've learned by now that there is a right way and a wrong way to express your displeasure. The former is likely to result in voluntary behavior adjustment. The latter in World War 7,235.

In my first book *PLAY NICE in Your Sandbox at Work,* I describe the XYZ technique, which gives a method to voice criticisms in a manner which will be well received and addressed. I've posted the chapter at my web page: PlayNiceinYourSandbox.com. You may find it there if you'd like. In the meantime, let me challenge you to throw away your list of your spouse's faults and add to your list of his or her positive attributes. It wouldn't hurt to spend a few moments each day looking over that list remembering why you chose to marry him or her in the first place.

A benefit of being grateful for what you have is that it protects you from becoming overly selfish and self-serving—both of which are dangerous in a marriage. I think we can all admit that as humans we tend to be self-centered, but marriage is an excellent opportunity to minimize that condition. By focusing on the positive aspects of your mate, you will be more inclined to consider how you might bring pleasure to him or her.

I heard a keynote speaker state that "love" in Greek means "look for the good." I'm certainly not a Greek scholar, but I don't think she's correct. I do appreciate the thought, though. To deepen and solidify the love in your home, why not spend some time looking for the good and expressing appropriate gratitude to and for your spouse and children? My hunch is you'll be well pleased with the results.

CHAPTER CHALLENGE

Take an honest look at your marriage and yourself. Do you put unrealistic expectations on your spouse and children and then get upset with them when they fail to live up to those expectations? Do you tend to focus more on their negative qualities than on their positive ones?

Here's a helpful habit you should form. Shortly after you awaken in the morning, take a few moments to write down on an index card five aspects of your spouse and children for which you are grateful. If you're feeling really industrious, consider putting their picture on the card. Carry the card with you, and pause at periodic moments in your day to pull out the card and read it. By the way, feel free to let your face know you are grateful—smiling has great health benefits.

DR. MIKE HATTABAUGH

In this video Dr. Hattabaugh talks about how the simple attribute of gratitude can greatly improve your chances for a healthy marriage.

**ProductiveOutcomes.com/
dr-mike-hattabaugh**

There is nothing wrong with your marriage if you're dealing with bills and kids and the broken garbage disposal and in-laws and work demands. That's a normal marriage.

—Dr. Phil McGraw

CHAPTER L1
When You Marry Jethro,
You Get the Clampetts

I SO WISH I COULD take credit for the title of this chapter. Come to think of it, there are a whole bunch of famous quotes I wish I could take credit for, but I'd best protect whatever credibility I might have and not do that. This quote comes from Dr. John Van Epp, author of *How to Avoid Falling in Love with a Jerk* and other relationship books.

In-laws are a vital component of most every marriage. According to marriage and family expert Dr. Kevin Leman, "It's not just two people who get married when they walk down the flower-strewn aisle, but at least six. And in the case of a stepfamily, it can be ten." He goes on to explain "The reason is that the person you marry is a result of how they were raised, good or bad. The influence has been from their parents, and perhaps more parents if they were part of a step-family."

First off, let me state for the record that I truly love and appreciate all of my wife's relatives. Some are easier to love at times, but look who is talking. People are people, and they are bound to get under your skin from time to time. In-laws just seem to have a special ability to do that more often than others. They can do it with such expertise you might think it was a goal in their life to make yours miserable.

A basic tenet for dealing with in-laws is identical to that when dealing with anyone else. Most people find that respect and the Golden Rule go a long way toward improving and maintaining healthy relationships. It would also help to realize that while these folks are not your blood relatives, they are your spouse's. I agree with Dr. Leman that a person is who they are largely due to the influence of these other relatives. In my opinion, in-laws deserve a special place of honor within your home. The habit of looking for the good should apply to them as well as to your spouse and children.

Having said that, may I make an earnest plea that you and your spouse come to terms on exactly what your in-laws' place should be. Once you make a commitment in marriage to forsake all others and to cleave (or join) only to each other, you are committing to putting your spouse and his or her needs above your other family members' needs.

Chapter LI

Balance is a requisite component in dealing with in-laws. I've dealt with many divorcing couples where one spouse forbade the other from having anything to do with his or her family. I'm at a loss to think of a good reason for this, but I can sure come up with a whole lot of bad ones.

You've heard the old expression that before you judge someone, you should walk a mile in their shoes—that way you'll be a mile away from them, and you'll have their shoes. Okay, another bad joke, but it is good advice when dealing with in-laws. Take some time to see yourself as they might see you. Might they see you as a thief who has stolen their son or daughter or brother or sister away? Might they see you as an intruder into what had previously been a happy, cohesive family?

So here's a thought for you in dealing with your in-laws, especially the mom and pop variety. Take a few moments and write them a thank-you note. Thank them for their sacrificial giving and nurturing and training, which resulted in the incredible person who has become your life partner. You don't need to go over the top, but the letter need not be skimpy, either. Because your spouse knows his or her folks better than you do, you might invite him or her to read it before you send it. This just helps to make sure the letter comes across as you intended, plus it might just earn you a point or two with your spouse—if you get my drift.

And one last thought on dealing with in-laws. Be respectful, but be united. If you are to succeed as a couple, it is vital that you not let anyone drive a wedge between you as in-laws will occasionally try to do. It is likely best for each spouse to address his or her own family if their family members are out of line in some respect. It is too difficult and awkward for one spouse to tell the other's parents that they are intrusive and/or offensive. But if your family attacks or demeans your spouse in any way, your immediate response must be to come to the defense of your spouse and let your family know such treatment will not be tolerated.

And just one last thought. Practice AGI with your in-laws. AGI stands for Assume Good Intent, which happens to be Chapter Three in my book *PLAY NICE in Your Sandbox at Work*. When you practice AGI, you give someone the benefit of the doubt that while he or she just hurt you, they likely didn't intend to. AGI allows you to stay calm and not automatically react or attack when someone does or says something you don't like.

You can likely admit there have been times in your life when you hurt someone inadvertently, but the damage was done. Would you have appreciated it if the other person gave you the benefit of the doubt that while you just messed up, you didn't mean to hurt them? We both know the answer is yes, so please make it a point to extend the same courtesy to others—including and perhaps especially your in-laws.

CHAPTER CHALLENGE

Make an effort to show appreciation to your in-laws this week. Consider writing the letter I suggested in the chapter, or get them a small gift, or use other means of letting them know you are glad to be a part of their family.

I've posted the chapter on AGI from PLAY NICE in Your Sandbox at Work on my website PlayNiceinYourSandbox.com. Take a moment to check it out and see how it might help you see the good in your in-laws and your other important relationships.

Courtesy is the one coin you can never have too much of or be stingy with.

—John Wanamaker

CHAPTER L2
Mind Your P's and T's

S OME YEARS AGO, MY wife and I had two other
couples over to our house for an enjoyable evening
of board games. One game was called Outburst, in
which you are challenged to rapidly call out ten items to
try to match those on a given list. The list might be foreign
cars or famous actors or books or whatever. The category
I most remember was "things your parents told you when
you were a child."

One of my partners, Rich Stimson, and I began to shout
out "Wash your hands before dinner" and "Don't talk with
your mouth full" and "Close the door; we don't live in a
barn" and, well, you get the picture. We were making good
progress toward the goal of ten, when all of a sudden our
other partner Erl Hendrickson blurted out "Shut up, or I'll
nail your other foot to the floor."

If you knew the usually calm and easygoing Erl, you would especially appreciate the shock and laughter that followed his contribution to the game. Needless to say, we did not score a point, as his suggestion was not one of the ten items listed. As I recall, neither Rich nor I could regain our composure to offer any more guesses before time expired for that round.

Just to remove any possible doubt in your mind, Erl was totally kidding, and neither he nor his parents would ever engage in such behavior. Calls to Child Protective Services were not appropriate or necessary. I recount this story for two reasons—actually, three.

The first reason is that it brings back a smile and great humor whenever I recall that event. The second reason is to remind you of the importance of keeping fun in your marriage and of having friends with whom to enjoy good times.

The third reason is to take a moment to recall one very important piece of advice, which most of our parents told us but which we may often neglect to put into practice. That would be to always say "please" and "thank you." I've noticed over the years in my marriage-coaching practice that couples who are in distress often forget these basic tenets of civility. Common courtesies that we extend to total strangers, we tend to withhold, at times, from those we love.

It's so easy in a family setting to take one another for granted. Without common courtesies, our requests can easily come across more as demands or expectations. There's an expression: "familiarity breeds contempt." Well, I guess that might be true in some circumstances and relationships. I think for marriage it is more likely that "familiarity breeds complacency." We somehow grow to feel our family members are stuck with us, so we no longer have to be nice to them.

While this practice may be common and easy to fall into, I've never seen it recommended in anyone's "how to do marriage" book. While I'm on a roll with expressions, I'll mention this one: "The grass is always greener on the other side of the fence." You suppose it might be because they take better care of their grass on the other side of the fence?

I often say that I hate the expression (another one?) that "marriage takes work." I work all day. I don't want to have to think about having to work all night as well. So rather than "marriage takes work," let me propose that "marriage takes determination and focus." Please don't fall into the habit of taking your loved ones for granted. Try saying "please" and "thank you" and "you're welcome," and any other courteous words you can think of, and I believe you'll find them well received.

One last reason why we may hesitate to use such words is the pressure we find ourselves under in these busy, hectic times. Many of us are overburdened with work issues, family issues, health issues, etc. From our reservoir of pain and distress, we can easily withhold civility from one another. I can't help you with the busyness other than to again suggest you read the book *Margin* by Dr. Richard Swenson.

In the meantime, let me remind you of one more bit of parental wisdom: "Mind your P's and Q's." I don't know what "P's" and "Q's" are, so I'll just suggest you mind your *P*'s (pleases) and *T*'s (thanks). And, by the way, thanks so much for reading this book.

CHAPTER CHALLENGE

Continue to practice the daily habit of looking for the good in your family members, but also look for opportunities to show your appreciation for them. Make note of their positive qualities and let them know how much you appreciate them. This may help you avoid ever taking them for granted.

To keep your marriage brimming,
with love in the wedding cup,
whenever you're wrong, admit it;
whenever you're right, shut up.

—Ogden Nash

SECTION THREE
PLAY NICE

Admit When You Are Wrong

I DON'T KNOW HOW MUCH you weigh, but I can give you a great weight-loss recommendation. You could quickly shed needless pounds through this one recommendation: take off the mask you have been wearing for several years.

In case I'm getting too personal, let me ask you to think of people you know who spend much of their time and energy trying to get others to believe they have it all together. While this might not actually add to their physical stature, I can promise you it takes a toll on their relationships and their outlook on life.

Please don't take what I'm saying too far. Some degree of self-protection is necessary and helpful to healthy relationships. We all need a healthy ego, an accurate, and positive self-image. But, like so many aspects of life, a good thing taken to an extreme becomes a bad thing. You likely know people for whom admitting they are wrong is difficult, if not impossible. A key component of a healthy ego, however, is the ability to admit when you are wrong and to accept any consequences connected to your wrong actions or behavior. So many problems in marriage could be avoided if one or both parties would suspend their efforts to "save face" and admit they did or said something inappropriate.

Dr. Mark Goulston, one of my all-time favorite authors (*Just Listen*; *Get Out of Your Own Way*; *Talking to Crazy*), observes that when people are verbally attacking one another, they are actually defending themselves from perceived attacks from the other. If that is true, and I believe it is, when either party stops the attack, the other can stop his or her defense and the battle can end. This "truce" would give the couple an opportunity to reasonably and rationally discuss whatever got them so upset in the first place. And, as Charles Herguth states: "Truce is better than friction."

Another book you might want to add to your library is *Daring Greatly* by Brené Brown. Ms. Brown makes the bold assertion that while most of us shun vulnerability at all costs, we should rather embrace and enjoy it. I consider that concept to be "R" rated in that it is not suitable for children.

Can you remember being around young children and being amused by their assertions that they are the "strongest," the "fastest," the "best?" These boasts are comical and harmless when coming from children. They are anything but comical and harmless when coming from someone who is supposed to have outgrown their childhood and become an adult.

Face it: we are all fragile and imperfect in some respects. Some people have gotten very good at hiding their vulnerability from others, and perhaps even from themselves. Such efforts make admitting when you have wronged someone difficult if not impossible.

It is a certainty in any close relationship that, over time, one party will hurt or disappoint the other. The only unknown is how long the impact of that mistreatment will last. The quickest way I know to lessen the time is to honestly admit your wrong, ask forgiveness, and move on.

I caution you, however, that for your admission to be accepted, it must be genuine. Please don't ever try to sugar coat your misdeeds. To say something like "If I wronged you" or "Maybe I hurt you, but . . ." is not likely to put the matter to rest. As the expression goes: "If you mess up, 'fess up!"

I read of a physics teacher who held out a cup of water and asked her students how heavy it was. The correct answer she received was not very heavy at all. She then asked her students how heavy it might be if she were to hold the cup for an hour or a day. Holding on to pride or ego and refusing to admit when you did wrong can get very heavy over time and take a serious toll on your relationship and happiness.

CHAPTER CHALLENGE

Learn to practice the fine art of humility and see what it does for your household harmony. Please don't go out of your way to hurt someone just so you can admit you did wrong, but you might want to look back to a time when you wronged your spouse or children and never admitted it. There likely is no better time than the present, so Nike, my friend: "Just do it!"

A successful marriage isn't the union of two perfect people. It's that of two imperfect people who have learned the value of forgiveness and grace.

—Darlene Schacht

CHAPTER A1
Don't Even Think About Trying This at Home

THE YEAR WAS **1970.** A movie came out with a slogan that swept the country. It permeated billboards, magazines, newspapers, TV, and radio. It seemed like one just could not escape hearing this endearing slogan.

Any guesses? . . . Time's up.

The movie was *Love Story*, and the slogan was (you or your parents know this one) "Love means never having to say you're sorry." Oh, isn't that so sweet. There's just one thing wrong with that idyllic concept: It's a bunch of nonsense. Love means frequently and regularly having to say you're sorry. This is especially true when love has led to marriage. Marriage is a union of two imperfect people who join together to try to form a perfect union. There will be times when you will step on each other's toes. Most of these times will be accidental, and a sincere apology quickly follows. Some of these times are intentional, and that's usually when an apology is most needed.

So rather than love and marriage being the lack of a need to say you're sorry, I propose that as Robert Quillen states, "A happy marriage is the union of two good forgivers." And marriage does indeed provide ample opportunities to practice and cultivate the art of forgiveness.

I appreciate the book *The Peacemaker* by Ken Sande. It's a Christian book with heavy emphasis on Bible teaching, so some of you may want to leave it on bookstore shelves. For those of you not averse to such teaching, it's a must-read. One particular thought he shares is much more realistic than the one from *Love Story*. He writes, "Unforgiveness is the poison we drink expecting the other person to die." That is so spot-on. When we refuse to forgive another, it is we who suffer far more than they. In fact, the other may be blissfully unaware that they are not forgiven in the first place. Yet we hold on to the attendant bitterness, anxiety, and negative thinking that accompanies a willful refusal to forgive.

Holding on to a grudge is akin to putting a pebble in your pocket. It's likely not going to pose a problem and will not impact you much at all, but what if the next day, you placed another pebble in your pocket and continued to add just one more on each succeeding day? Over time, you would find yourself greatly impacted and debilitated by the weight you were carrying around.

This is still a free country, and you are entitled to withhold forgiveness from someone who has wronged you. I invite you to count the cost, however, and decide if that's really what you want to do.

To forgive, by the way, is not the same as to forget. Another well-known expression that sounds good on the surface, but which has a deadly flaw, is "forgive and forget." What, you may ask, is wrong with that? Simply that it is impossible. Stop for a moment and think of your kindergarten or first-grade teacher. I find that most people can quickly bring to mind the name and face of someone they had not thought of in years—decades, in fact.

The point I'm making is that our minds, unless damaged in some way, retain every experience, every moment of our lives. Therefore, to try to forget a past hurt or wrong is just not possible. It's not a matter of forgive and forget as much as it is forgive and move on or forgive and let it go.

You might not be able to control the emotional component of your resentment or bitterness, but you can certainly choose not to act on those emotions. Over time, it gets easier and easier to truly move beyond the hurt or offense. So, while the forgetting part is not possible, the forgiving part is, and I highly recommend you consider doing so—particularly if the one needing forgiveness is your spouse.

To be clear, by "move on," I do not suggest you must leave the relationship with the offender—especially if you are married to him or her. By "move on" I mean that you go forward, leaving the past in the past. I often see folks in my office trying to move forward with both hands holding tenaciously to the past. If you ever find a way to do that successfully, please let me know, because I've not yet figured out how it can be done. I think it helps to think of forgiveness as a decision rather than an emotion. And it is a decision you make for yourself as much—or perhaps even more than—for the benefit of the other person.

To forgive is also not to say you weren't indeed hurt that badly in the first place. The damage and pain can be severe, but you can decide that it is in the past and not let it dominate your thoughts and treatment of the other in the present or future. I realize this may be easier for some than for others. Some have been hurt so deeply that it will be a real struggle to choose to forgive. Please never forget, however, that you are a free moral agent and you really can choose to forgive if you want to.

Oh, I can hear some of you now saying, "Yeah, but you don't realize what he/she did to me!" Actually, I do know. Not the specifics, of course, but in 29+ years of divorce mediation and 17+ years of marriage coaching, I have heard my share of horrific treatment experienced by one spouse at the hands of the other.

At the top of my list is the time I mediated a divorce resulting from the discovery that on the night before their wedding, the groom slept with the bride's sister and got her pregnant. Of course, they didn't know she was pregnant, so the wedding went on as scheduled, and during the honeymoon, the bride became pregnant. What joy for sisters to be pregnant at the same time—until they realized it was by the same father. How'd you like to go to those family reunions?

Trust me, I could go on with horror stories of cruel and unusual punishment I have heard from couples, but I will spare you the gory details. I'm confident that you or someone close to you has a troublesome story to tell. And, while we cannot go back and undo the damage, fortunately, we can minimize the effects. And the best way I know to do that is to give as total and complete forgiveness as you are able. Not always easy, I grant you, but just about always the best course to take.

Please realize that forgiveness does not mean that you think what the other did to you is just fine or even that you have to remain in relationship with that person. Some hurts are too deep to be able to overcome and risk reoccurrence.

Forgiveness simply means you are canceling the debt owed to you and you wish no harm to come to the offender. You determine to leave the hurt in the past and never mention it again. You determine that when the thought of the hurt comes to your mind, you will quickly and decisively refuse to act upon it.

I heard of a woman who had been deeply hurt by another woman, but she decided she would forgive her. When a friend heard she had decided to forgive, she asked "How can you forgive—don't you remember what she did to you?" to which the woman replied, "No, I specifically remember forgetting that." I just love that line: "I specifically remember forgetting that." While this is certainly an oxymoron, it is quite possible to take control of any thoughts of vengeance or hostility in deference to your decision to forgive and move on.

It's a sad reality that withholding forgiveness has led to many divorces that likely could have been prevented. I am not one to judge or to say that anyone who has gotten a divorce is a terrible person. There are certainly times when divorce is right and appropriate. It's extremely rare, however, that divorce is the best first option.

CHAPTER CHALLENGE

Granting forgiveness to someone who has hurt you deeply can be difficult. I encourage you to make the decision and day by day act on that decision until your feelings catch up with your thoughts. If you feel you cannot forgive by yourself, please consider getting help from a spiritual advisor or mental health provider or relationship coach. I'm confident that any such efforts will be well worth the investment.

The pessimist complains about the wind; the optimist expects it to change; the realist adjusts the sails.

—**William Arthur Ward**

CHAPTER A2
Change for the Better?

THERE'S AN OLD EXPRESSION that a rut is just a grave with openings on each end. True or not, your marriage can easily fall into the form of ruts if you're not careful to keep that from happening. Most people will admit that change is difficult, but so is trying to resist change. I've heard it said that people do not actually resist change nearly as much as they resist being changed. I think there's a lot of truth in that statement. I've also heard it said that a woman marries a man hoping he will change and a man marries a woman hoping she never will. I'm not so sure I agree with that one, but it's likely true in some cases.

The point I hope to make in this chapter is that trying to change your mate is wasted energy at best and highly toxic to the relationship at worst. While dangerous to the overall health of the relationship, attempts to change one's partner are very common in marriage. Such attempts are often well motivated from a deep sense of love, care, and genuine concern. But when you're on the receiving end of such attempts, they do not come across as well intended, no matter how much they may actually be.

If you are the requestor of the change, you are likely thinking about all the potential benefits to your spouse and/or to your marriage that will result from your suggested changes. If you are on the receiving end, however, you are likely hearing that your mate is not pleased with you or how you are doing life at the moment and that he/she wants you to change not just *what you do* but *who you are*.

As is the case in so much of life, right intentions and motivations do not always gain the desired results. So let me give you a piece of advice which might make change in your spouse more likely to occur. That advice is to change yourself first in ways that he or she is likely to notice and appreciate.

Have you ever noticed that often when you are upset with your mate, it is because you are already upset about something else? How often do children pay the price for how poorly their moms or dads were treated at work that day?

The next time you find yourself perturbed with your mate, you might want to stop and examine whether he or she is the true cause of your agitation. You may realize you are upset because you didn't sleep well the night before, or because you're hungry, or because a pressing problem is weighing heavily on you or . . . You've likely heard the expression that negative emotions often arise from feeling H.A.L.T. (Hungry, Angry, Lonely, or Tired). I like what Mark Twain said: "The worst loneliness is not to be comfortable with yourself."

Another truth I have picked up along life's journey is that often the changes you desire for your mate are actually changes you desire in yourself, but somehow seem unable to accomplish. You want to start an exercise program, so you get down on him or her because he or she doesn't. You want to eat a more healthful diet, so you get upset when your mate brings home junk food. You want to reduce the amount of garbage you put into your mind, so you get upset when he or she watches questionable television programs or movies.

Numerous other illustrations abound, but I think you get my point. You resent it when people try to force changes on you, so please give up the notion that your mate is going to appreciate when you do the same to him or her.

So am I suggesting that when you see your mate engaging in self-destructive behaviors, you simply stand by and do nothing? I hope not. What I am suggesting is that you do what Mahatma Gandhi is alleged to have said: "Be the change you desire to see in the world" or, in this case, your marriage. There is some dispute about whether this is in fact what he actually said, but the sentiment of the thought is still valid nonetheless, especially perhaps as it applies to marriage.

So often, each spouse waits for the other to change before he or she is willing to make improvements in the marriage. Rather than waiting for your spouse, may I suggest you consider taking the initiative to be the change you want to see in your marriage.

I remember watching the *TODAY Show* several years ago. I was about to turn it off and go back to work when I heard that the next segment would feature an animal trainer who used animal training techniques to train her husband. Needless to say, this piqued my interest enough to stay tuned. While I can't remember the guest's name, I will never forget her words.

She told of techniques used in animal training whereby you look for the behavior you want from the animal, and you lavish praise and rewards each time you see that behavior. Rather than look for what you don't want and criticize, she admonished, it is far better to look for the good and to recognize it appropriately. So she decided to stop criticizing her husband and to make a determined effort to thank and appreciate him for what he did to contribute to the household and the marriage.

As she concluded her segment, she told the interviewer that her husband responded very positively to her new approach. She stated, "He really changed." Her final words were in the form of a rhetorical question: "Or was it I who really changed?" While I've never considered myself to be much of a dancer, I can assure you I did a joyful jig in my office when I heard those words that morning. And how true it is that one person can dramatically turn a marriage around.

Will this be quick? I didn't say that. Will it be easy? I didn't say that, either. But will it be worth it for you to make changes in how you treat your spouse in hopes the relationship will improve? Only you can answer that, but in most cases, the answer should be a resounding YES!

Along with being less critical and more encouraging, let me share with you a few other ideas to help make your marriage happier and healthier. My first suggestion comes from the movie, *Fireproof*, starring Kirk Cameron and a whole bunch of folks you've never heard of. Mr. Cameron plays the part of a firefighter whose marriage is falling apart. At first, he doesn't care but then realizes what he is doing to contribute to its impending demise. His father gives him a book titled *The Love Dare*, which is a 40-day challenge to improve the quality of a marriage.

Each day lists a specific exercise to reach out to your mate in a loving fashion. The exercises are designed to help your mate know how you feel and how much you value him or her and your relationship. Trust me when I tell you it's not all that easy to keep to the schedule, especially as some days' exercises are more involved than others. I teamed up with a friend to take the Love Dare for our wives and hold each other accountable. I believe it took us some 60 days or so, but we eventually did, as they say, "Get 'er done."

I would share with you the results of this experience on my marriage, but frankly that's just none of your business. You can get your own copy of *The Love Dare* by Alex Kendrick and Stephen Kendrick online or at a local bookstore and find out for yourself what might happen. While not easy, I can assure you that taking the time and spending the energy to help your mate feel appreciated by you will be well worth the investment.

A second suggestion comes from Dr. Scott Stanley, esteemed marriage and family researcher, and co-founder of PREP Inc. Dr. Stanley suggests you consider two things your mate would appreciate receiving from you. These can be actual gifts or simple tokens of affection that he or she would enjoy receiving. Your task, obviously, is to make the time to deliver, each week, whatever you've chosen as your intentional demonstrations of love.

What do you suppose would be the impact on marriages if both spouses were to form the habit of giving their partner two purposeful love gestures each week? My hunch is that it would be fun to find out.

You may have heard of the immortal words of John F. Kennedy, our 35th president, who said at his inauguration, "Ask not what your country can do for you; ask what you can do for your country." Again, with only a slight revision, this is wise wisdom to apply to your marriage: "Ask not what your spouse can do for you; ask what you can do for your spouse."

Will any of these suggestions bring guaranteed results? I can't make such a declaration. But, if you'll permit me one last quote, I'll turn once again to my Jewish grandmother who often said, "it couldn't hurt."

CHAPTER CHALLENGE

Determine to take personal responsibility for the state of your marriage. As you begin to make changes in yourself and pay more attention to your marriage, you are likely to find a reciprocal response from your mate—in time. Please note, I said, "in time." You must demonstrate your change before your mate is likely to follow suit. And even if he or she doesn't change, you will be better for your efforts.

*There are
all kinds of
addicts, I guess.
We all have
pain. And we
all look for ways
to make the
pain go away.*

—Sherman Alexie

CHAPTER A3
Addictions Destroy Marriages

WE'RE FUNNY CREATURES, WE humans. We have our good points and our not-so-good points. The same may be said for our marriages. Sometimes we are doing great, and we feel like Leonardo DiCaprio in his famous line from the movie *Titanic*: "I'm king of the world!" Other times we feel like "the biggest loser."

What makes the difference? Well, there are lots of possible explanations, some common and some more unique to one's individual circumstances. One common threat to marriage which I have observed in my coaching career is addictions, where one, or perhaps both, spouses are trapped by something that steals time and energy from their marriage.

Some of the more common addictions are pornography, video games, TV, Facebook, food, drugs, and alcohol, etc. Now it is certainly not my place to judge, but I am confident in saying that if any of these (or others you may substitute) have become more important to you than your spouse and your marriage, you must deal with them rigorously and soon.

I do not claim to be an expert in addiction recovery, but I do know that addictions develop over a period of time through repeated use and practice. The very good news is that they can be replaced by better options through the same process of time and repetition.

Addictions may be thought of as habits which we routinely do without much thought or consideration. Habits are often thought of in the negative sense, but actually, the creation and implementation of good habits can have a dramatically powerful and helpful impact on your life and your marriage.

Take, for example, forming the habit of saying "I love you" frequently and regularly. How about forming the habit of leaving little notes of support and encouragement around your home or having them sent to your spouse's workplace?

Why not form the habit of having regular date nights together each week, or at least every other week at a minimum?

I encourage all of my clients to form the habit of calling a time-out (See Chapter Y3) when one or both are too upset to engage in a positive conversation. Calling a time-out can help you avoid situations that you will likely regret later on.

There are many more positive habits that you could put into practice, and I've listed some in other chapters. For now, however, I want to return to the negative habits, or addictions, which can devastate a marriage—and a life, for that matter.

Each of the negative addictions I cited above is deserving of an entire chapter of its own. So many men are addicted to pornography, and by any measure you use, it is just wrong and indefensible. I've heard horror stories of men who make love to their wives with a Playboy centerfold lying in the bed beside them. I can't begin to imagine how degrading, insensitive, and hurtful that must be to those women, who might already have doubts about their beauty and self-worth.

It boggles my mind the hours that some can spend engaged in video games to the total exclusion of their spouse and children. I can understand the thrill and draw of such activities, but the regret and loneliness faced in later years when you are divorced and your children want nothing to do with you will hardly equal the temporary moments of joy and exhilaration.

TV is a fixture in most every home. Hundreds and hundreds of programs to choose from add up to hundreds and hundreds of hours of drifting apart from each other. Some marriage experts suggest that newlywed couples not own a TV the first year of their marriage. This will help them learn to connect and engage in more marriage-building activities. My wife and I followed this suggestion and can personally attest to its benefit.

Facebook, while having a positive impact in helping folks to reconnect with friends from years gone by, has also been instrumental in contributing to numerous affairs and divorce. If you're not careful, it can take over your life.

Food addictions are often an indicator of underlying physical, mental, or emotional disturbance, which extra food is woefully inadequate to resolve. Counseling and therapy are available and might be required to successfully overcome a food addiction. The same may be said for any other addiction as well. There should be no shame or hesitancy in admitting you have a problem that you cannot defeat on your own. All of us can benefit from a "checkup from the neck up" every once in a while.

And, lastly, drugs and alcohol have likely torn apart more marriages and families than any other type of addiction or threat. There are usually reasons why people escape into such substances, but rarely are they good reasons. And rarely does the escape truly address the underlying problem or issue.

As with all addictions, help is available to those who will admit they need the help and who are willing to seek it. There is likely a chapter of Alcoholics Anonymous, Narcotics Anonymous, or other organization in your area waiting for you to ask for help. Al-Anon is available for the spouse of one caught in addictions. Celebrate Recovery is a Christian-based program designed to address drug, alcohol, and other disruptive addictions. Participants also find help to address emotional and spiritual concerns.

If you or a loved one is struggling to overcome an addiction, let me suggest you determine that you will fight the fight together.

My closing thought is that if your marriage or your life is not working the way you would like, if it's not clicking on all cylinders, then please don't give up. Seek the appropriate support, and you just might be amazed at how much better things can be.

CHAPTER CHALLENGE

Look into resources in your area and schedule a time to participate together—if that's allowed. Discussing sensitive topics such as addictions can be tricky. You have my permission to jump ahead to Chapter Y2 to learn how to use the LUV talk that's listed there. Rather than condemning or fault-finding, offer your mate your care, concern, and willingness to join them in the battle.

*A good marriage
is a contest of
generosity.*

—Diane Sawyer

Section Four
PLAY NICE

Yield:
It's a great investment strategy

I HAD THE PRIVILEGE OF preparing a couple for marriage, and of performing the wedding ceremony in which they made lifelong commitments to each other. Since I am seemingly incapable of doing anything without humor, I suggested to them that by getting married, they were giving up certain rights. As an example, I explained that they were now giving up their right to "life, liberty, and the pursuit of happiness." I shall never forget the look on the bride's face. Behind the abject horror was a sincere hope that I was kidding—which I certainly was.

I went on to explain that marriage is not like eating at Burger King. For those of you too young to remember, the Burger King Company ran an ad campaign in the 1970s that proclaimed at their restaurant you could always "have it your way." While that might work at a fast-food restaurant, I assured the couple before me, as I assure you, the reader: this is not always the case in marriage, nor should it be.

While you certainly have the right to determine if, when, and to whom you might get married, once that decision is made, you voluntarily relinquish your right to make future decisions by and for yourself alone. For a marriage to be successful, the partners must have a mindset of "we" rather than "me." Having said that, I have a personal pet peeve against the practice of extinguishing each spouse's individual candle after they have jointly lit the unity candle. I understand the symbolism, but feel it can be taken too far.

When you marry, you do not have to abandon who you are and join with your partner to form an enmeshed blob. That is just not healthy for the parties or the marriage. You do, however, need to realize that as a married person, your identity will and should change. Marriage is a special relationship unlike any other known to man, in which two people form a bond, determined that they shall go through life together as an "us."

By definition, therefore, there will be times when each partner will have to yield to the wishes and concerns of the other. I say "have to," but what would your marriage be like if each of you chose to yield, not so much as an obligation, but as a gesture of love and caring?

In his faith-based book *Sacred Marriage*, Gary Thomas asks, "What if God designed marriage to make us Holy more than to make us happy?" Marriage is a wonderful living laboratory in which we may practice selfless love. It is not always easy, but frequent demonstrations of self-sacrificing love usually pay huge dividends and bode well for a long, satisfying marriage.

Again, there will be times in every marriage when each spouse will need to yield his or her preferences to those of his or her spouse. But what do you do when each spouse feels strongly about how a particular matter should be resolved? One way to determine the situation is to ask each one "on a scale of 1–10, how important is it that we do what you are asking?" This calls for honesty on each person's part. You cannot simply say "10" every time the question is raised. Typically, one partner will feel more deeply about the issue than the other, and his or her preference should prevail. In a healthy marriage, these situations will balance out over time.

I'll leave you with one more suggestion to get around apparent gridlocks in your marriage. My wife and I met and married in Cortez, Colorado. Five years into our marriage, I had a strong desire for us to move to Farmington, New Mexico, about 70 miles away from Cortez. I broached the subject to my wife and quickly realized she did not share my enthusiasm in the least. To be fair, I must tell you that my wife was born and raised in Cortez and that her mother and sister still resided there. Her roots went deep, and she did not want to entertain the thought of a "root canal." I decided to drop the matter.

A few months later, I again asked my wife to consider agreeing to let me move us to Farmington, and again she made it abundantly clear that she did not want to do that. I dropped the matter once again, but only for a few more weeks. I then explained to her that I realized I did not have the right to demand that we move to Farmington, but neither did she have the right to deny the move. Since the "irresistible force" (my desire to relocate) met up with the "immovable object" (her desire to stay), I proposed a middle position.

I explained in depth why I felt so strongly that a move would be in "our" best interest and then gave her an offer she could not refuse. I suggested she give me the next year of our marriage and allow me to move us to Farmington. Whatever happened, she would have the next year and could move us back to Cortez if she wished. She asked if I was serious and after assuring her I was, I sweetened the deal. Knowing how close she was to her mother, I assured her that if she consented to the move, I would never ask her to move further away from her mother than the 70 miles that Farmington is from Cortez.

I'm not sure if I finally wore down her resistance, or she simply accepted the reasonableness of my offer, but in either event, we are still contented residents of Farmington as we enter our 38th year of marriage.

You've heard the expression "give and take." I propose you adopt the mindset of "give and give." When each party goes out of his or her way to yield to the other, the taking will take care of itself.

CHAPTER CHALLENGE

Spend some time this week looking at your marriage from your mate's point of view. Look for opportunities to put your own needs and desires aside to better meet those of your spouse. A great resource to help you do this is called *The Love Dare* from the movie *Fireproof*, which I referenced in Chapter A2. It's available at thelovedarebook.com and other book outlets.

DR. MARK GOULSTON

I'm willing to wager you have never heard of Mediated Catharsis, but in this short clip Dr. Mark Goulston will give you an excellent tool to stop arguments in their tracks.

**ProductiveOutcomes.com/
dr-mark-goulston**

The single biggest problem in communication is the illusion that it has taken place.

—George Bernard Shaw

CHAPTER Y1
You Simply Cannot Fail at This!

PEOPLE OF MY GENERATION well remember the famous quote uttered by Strother Martin in his role as a prison warden in the 1967 film *Cool Hand Luke*. It was addressed to Paul Newman, and according to Wikipedia the phrase is "#11 on the American Film Institute list, AFI's 100 Years . . . 100 Movie Quotes." The phrase to which I refer is "What we've got here is [a] failure to communicate."

While these words may be a blast from the past, trust me when I tell you I hear them just about every day in my marriage-coaching practice. When couples come to me seeking improvements in their relationship, I ask them to tell me two or three things that are "broken" in their relationship which they would like to see "repaired." I haven't kept statistics, but I'm thinking 99.99% of the couples cite poor communication as one of their presenting problems. Typically it is listed first, and typically it's cited by both spouses.

This shouldn't come as a great surprise, since few of us were ever taught how to communicate in relationships. For most couples, in the early days of getting acquainted, communication flows so naturally and easily that they make the mistake of believing it will always be that way and no additional training is necessary. Unfortunately, they soon discover the inaccuracy of this prediction. When communication works well, life is great, but when it's off, the relationship can be in great peril.

According to Nancy Landrum, co-author with her late husband Jim, of *How To Stay Married and Love It!*, "Poor communication is cited as one of the most common causes of divorce. Even when other reasons are given, the inability to communicate effectively often exacerbates the issues rather than helping to resolve them. Lack of effective communication creates a sense of isolation, frustration, and disconnection."

In their book, Nancy and Jim give a fairly extensive list of ways you should not communicate. They term the following "Defective Communication Tools," and I absolutely recommend you avoid these at all cost. Just for fun, you might want to grab a sheet of paper and honestly check off those that you frequently do and those which you feel your partner frequently does:

☐ use *always* and *never* statements

☐ give unwanted advice

☐ use the silent treatment

☐ use sarcasm

☐ act like a martyr or victim

☐ slam doors or throw things

☐ compare your spouse to someone else

☐ embarrass your spouse in public

☐ use threats or other controlling behaviors

☐ jab with "zingers" (Try to tell me you don't know what those are.)

☐ talk in a condescending tone

☐ yell, scream, or rage

☐ bring others into your disagreement

☐ withhold sex or affection

☐ defend and make excuses

☐ blame and use an accusatory tone

Well, the list can go on, but I think you get the idea. The point is that we all develop bad habits over time, and poor communication habits are no exception. Very few of us are expert communicators 100% of the time. That even goes for folks who are supposed to be professional communicators, but please don't ask me how I know that.

It's also true that old habits can be hard to break, but I suggest you look over the above list of negatives and choose one or two that you will be willing to focus on and practice eliminating from your verbal repertoire.

Again, because change can be difficult, let me offer you two pointers to consider. One, consider what you do want to do differently rather than focus on what you're trying not to do. I don't fully understand the brain science, but I've been told that the brain does not hear the word "don't."

For instance, if you tell a child, "Don't spill your milk" his or her brain will hear, "Spill your milk," and you can pretty well guess what will happen next. This seems to hold true for adults as well. We are far better suited to accomplish what we do want rather than avoiding what we don't. So choose an old communication habit or two you would like to change and focus your energy on practicing the intended behavior.

My second suggestion is that you solicit help from your spouse in breaking the old ways and replacing them with new. Simply tell him or her what you are trying to do differently and that if they ever catch you falling back to the old ways, they are not to say anything or react in any manner. What they are to do is hold out their hand, and you are required to fill it with a $1.00 bill, or perhaps a $5 or $10 bill as a fine.

The idea here is not a new money-making scheme, but rather to implement a gentle, often comical, reminder that you have chosen to forgo the old ways of communicating and to replace them with the new. You could even invite your children to participate, but be prepared for them to try to trick you at times to be able to catch you in the act.

Folks, if you are married, you are a team. You are in this wonderful adventure of life together, and the ability to communicate is and should be one that you learn how to do well. Effective communication is a tremendous asset in helping each partner yield to the other. By truly listening to each other and speaking appropriately each will feel validated and honored in the relationship. Nobody ever said it would be easy, but I can assure you the benefits are well worth the effort required.

CHAPTER CHALLENGE

Because effective communication
is such an important component of
a healthy marriage, I address other
aspects of it in the coming chapters,
so keep reading. You might also want
to get a book on communication
(some are listed in the resource
section) and read it together as
a couple.

Avoid miscommunication. The price you pay for it is horrendous.

—Shiv Khera

CHAPTER Y2
SLT? LUV?
Call it What You Will—Just do It!

DID YOU HEAR ABOUT the lady who went to an attorney for help in divorcing her husband? The attorney, seeking to understand her reasons for getting divorced, asked her if she had grounds. "Oh yes," she replied, "probably two or three acres." Realizing she had misunderstood his question, the attorney asked her if she wanted a divorce because she had a grudge, to which she replied, "No, only a carport." Fighting his exasperation, he tried once more and asked if her husband ever beat her up. She answered, "Oh, no, I'm always up before he is." Finally, he just asked her outright, "Ma'am, why do you want to divorce this man?" Her reply? "Because there's just no way I can communicate with him."

I think that's pretty funny and it reminds me that, as I wrote in the previous chapter, over 90% of the couples who come to me for marriage coaching list inability to communicate as the major factor in their troubled relationship. This should come as no surprise since communication with people, in general, can be challenging at times. Doesn't it stand to reason that miscommunication will occur with someone in whose company you find yourself a great deal of the time?

It's important to realize that each of us has a deeply felt need to be understood. We've had this drive since infancy, and it does not diminish over time. What happens in so many homes is that each person is trying to be understood at the same time. Well, if both people are talking, then who is listening? And if no one is listening, who is understanding? Make sense?

Many couples fall into the trap of each wanting more to be understood than they are interested in understanding their mate. I've heard this referred to as the "shoot and reload" method of communicating, where each party listens more to what he or she is thinking than to what the other is actually saying. Or, as French playwright Albert Guinon put it, "There are people who, instead of listening to what is being said to them, are already listening to what they are going to say themselves."

Another hindrance to effective communication is the commonly held fear that by listening and understanding the other, you may be misinterpreted as also agreeing with the other. Wrong! You did not marry your clone—at least I hope you didn't. You will disagree on many issues, both large and small. This is normal and actually healthy for the relationship if you grow to appreciate your differences.

The very simple, though not always easy, remedy is to have one person speak while the other just listens and then take turns in each role. This technique goes by various titles. The Covey Seven Habits for Highly Effective People course uses the Talking Stick to determine which role each person has at the time. The speaker obviously has the stick. I am so tempted to say, "No sticky, no speaky," but I will refrain.

The Talking Stick is from Habit Five—Seek First to Understand, Then to be Understood. This is a wonderful principle for all of life and especially, perhaps, marriage. Often in life, we make matters a competition and, while this may be fine for sporting events or chess games, it is not a good practice for marriage. So long as both parties get to be understood, what difference does it make who goes first?

The creators of PREP have popularized a method of communication that promotes understanding and emotional safety while inhibiting nasty conflicts. In their books such as *Fighting for Your Marriage* and *A Lasting Promise*, Howard Markman, Scott Stanley, and their colleagues use the term the "Speaker–Listener Technique" to describe their method, which clearly delineates who is speaking and who is listening. Instead of a Talking Stick, they implement the "Floor" principle as in whoever has the floor has the right to speak and be understood.

The late Gary Smalley, a longtime warrior in the battle to enhance marriage, was influenced by Stanley and Markman, and taught "LUV Talk." LUV stands for Listen, Understand, Validate, and trust me, it is highly validating to your spouse when you truly listen to him or her without agreeing, disagreeing, or judging in any way.

Effective communication in marriage is fairly simple, yet not always easy. There are many reasons for this, among them the presence of communication filters whereby you don't necessarily hear what your spouse intends to say. Many of us have taken speech classes at some point in our educational career, but how many of us have been trained to listen?

Most of us can hear with little or no difficulty, so we tend to think that listening requires no special effort or attention. In a word, that's just WRONG! Sorry for shouting, but I wanted to make sure you heard me. Our minds are going all the time, and if we don't make a determined effort to focus them, they will run wild with distractions. That's where the Talking Stick or Floor Card come in. They help to slow things down and keep the focus on the communication at hand, rather than on a myriad of other thoughts.

There are simple rules for this method of effective communication. First, you determine who will be the speaker and who will be the listener. The speaker holds the Floor Card or Talking Stick. It doesn't matter what implement you use so long as both of you agree to and adhere to its designated function. If you're out at a restaurant, a coffee mug or salt shaker could serve the purpose. You'll be passing it back and forth, so I don't recommend you use knives or forks until you master the technique.

Rule number one for the speaker is that he or she must speak for him or herself and avoid mind-reading at all costs. It is quite insulting to be told what you are thinking, especially because the one who is guessing is usually inaccurate. Well, if you don't like someone assuming they can read your mind, perhaps it's a good idea to refrain from doing it to someone else?

Rule number two for the speaker is to keep your statements brief—not go on and on. The purpose of engaging in the LUV Talk is to achieve understanding, unlike the Shoot and Reload method, in which persuasion is the primary goal. By keeping your statements brief, you can put into practice rule number three, which is to stop and let the listener paraphrase.

Again, if your goal is to convince your partner that you are right and he or she is wrong, then simply keep talking and never stop. But if you truly want them to understand, and to know that they understand accurately, you must give them a chance to tell you what they have heard you say.

Paraphrasing calls upon the listener to state in his or her own words what he or she has heard, without agreeing, disagreeing, or qualifying in any way. Paraphrasing is not simply parroting back the speaker's words. That just demonstrates an ability to memorize words—it does not indicate understanding. By putting in your own words what you believe the other has said, both parties can determine whether what was said is actually what was heard and if understanding has taken place.

There are just two rules for the listener, but they are vital to the overall success of the process. Rule number one is to paraphrase what you hear, which I hope I've sufficiently covered. This is often easier said than done. We humans are able to think at a far greater speed than most people can speak. Therefore, we often listen to our own thoughts in addition to, or instead of, the other person's voice. To truly listen well, you must turn off your inner voice and totally focus on what is being said to you. Knowing that there will be a quiz should help motivate you to pay attention.

The second rule for the listener is to focus on the speaker's message and not rebut. Here's where it can get dicey. So often, when we hear something we don't agree with, we want to jump in and immediately correct the error. Again, that's fine if you really don't care about the relationship and you just want to be victorious over your partner. I suggest it is far more effective and productive to fully hear what the other is saying and save your rebuttal for when you have the floor.

And, finally, there are rules for both. The first rule is that the speaker has the floor and he or she is the only one who can speak. If you don't have the floor, you simply wait your turn and put your full attention on the message coming your way.

There will be times when the listener is verbalizing what he or she heard from the speaker. But, because he or she can only state what they heard from the speaker, the speaker retains control of the floor as he or she is still in the role of speaker. If the paraphrase indicates understanding has not occurred, the speaker simply tries again. Once understanding has been demonstrated, the speaker may add additional information or pass the floor as he or she prefers.

The final rule for both is that the parties share the floor. This is a conversation conducted as two separate monologues. It is vital that each person has a chance to be listened to and understood.

I urge you to give the Floor/LUV Talk a try. You'll likely stumble at first and interrupt or try to over talk your mate, but with practice, my hunch is you'll get really good at communicating—even in delicate areas. In fact, the LUV Talk should only be used in sensitive matters when emotions are present and misunderstanding likely to occur. It is not necessary—or helpful—in everyday conversations.

If you are on a road trip and your wife asks you to stop at the next rest stop, please refrain from saying, "So

I understand you to say your bladder has become fully engorged and you would like to alleviate that situation at the next convenient moment." You will have shown understanding but likely will not get an appreciative response. Or if your husband comes home and says, "Would you like to go out to dinner?" don't you dare say "I understand you to say that there is a cavernous emptiness within your belly and you would like to satiate that emptiness with food from a public establishment designated for that purpose." Your much better reply would be, "Absolutely. Where should we go?"

I cannot emphasize strongly enough, however, that if the conversation involves matters which are difficult to discuss for any reason, or are sensitive and painful, you would be wise to use some version of The Speaker-Listener Technique. You might think that all sounds unnatural, but like Scott Stanley often asks, "Tell me again what you two naturally do with difficult conversations? Natural is overrated." The risks to the relationship are just too high not to do something that can help you slow down and understand each other when something important is at stake. In the words of John Powell, "Communication works for those who work at it."

Along with not working on their communication, far too many couples never work on their marriage at all. They put little or no effort into learning how to do it better, and so they come to a place where they lose hope that they can ever be a happy couple again. Please don't let this happen to you or to someone you know.

I'll leave you with one last communication tip, which is especially helpful in avoiding potentially heated discussions. It comes from the Family Life organization out of

Little Rock, Arkansas, and concerned a couple who often argued over money—not exactly a rarity in our day. They realized that financial conversations typically turned ugly, so they decided to take three-inch square Post-It notes and write on them, "I am not the enemy!" They would then post these notes on their foreheads before entering into the conversation. Silly? Probably so. But effective? Why not try it for yourself and find out.

CHAPTER CHALLENGE

If you want to learn more about the Speaker Listener Technique and other helpful skills from PREP, check out their online program for couples at lovetakeslearning.com. PREP offers many other marriage classes and resources you might enjoy. Visit PREPInc.com to see if there is a class in your area, or near someone you know should attend. You might also look for the Floor Card and order a magnetized version to post on your refrigerator.

A successful marriage is an edifice that must be rebuilt every day.

—**Andre Maurois**

CHAPTER Y3
A Pause that Refreshes

THERE IS A WOMAN in our country who is brilliant, but she is rarely given credit for her intelligence and wisdom. The woman to whom I refer is Paris Hilton who once told an interviewer that she was "not a rocket surgeon." I so want to believe she said that on purpose just to be funny, but I'm not sure. At any rate, I am happy to tell you that successful marriage is not a matter of "rocket surgery."

If couples would simply master a few key practices and implement them on a regular basis, they could expect to succeed as a couple. One such key practice is to form the habit of calling a time-out when one or both are too upset to carry on a civil conversation. It should come as no surprise that this is yet another valuable tool I learned in my PREP training. Relationship experts Markman and Stanley both teach that if there was only one skill from all of what they teach in PREP that they'd want every couple to master, it's this one.[3]

I cannot overemphasize the importance of this practice. So often in a marriage, or any other close relationship, we can easily become so upset that we are capable of inflicting great harm on someone we care about. All too often, the harm is of a physical nature, which is flat-out wrong and unacceptable in any circumstance. Most often, the harm is emotional, which can often be even more painful and longer lasting than the physical.

The old expression "I was so mad I couldn't think straight" is literally and physiologically true. Your ability to have a civil, constructive conversation when you or your spouse is agitated and upset is virtually nil—so don't even try. Call a time-out and schedule a time to meet up later when cooler heads might prevail.

There will be times when one or both of you will simply not be at your best. Times when even the most beautiful and handsome of us can become downright ugly. Trust me, those are not times when you want to engage in a discussion. It will not go well; I can just about guarantee it. I often suggest to my clients that there have likely been times in their marriage when they were acting like little children sticking their tongues out at each other and stomping their

3 Markman, H. J., Stanley, S. M., & Blumberg, S. L. (2010). Fighting for your marriage. San Francisco: Jossey-Bass.

Stanley, S., Trathen, D., McCain, S., & Bryan, M. (2014). A lasting promise: The Christian Guide to Fighting for Your Marriage. San Francisco: Jossey Bass, Inc.

feet. I typically act this out, which evokes laughter from them. Their laughter, I have learned, is usually an admission of recognition and guilt. I then ask them to recall for me a time when it was productive that they engaged in such hurtful and childish discourse. I have yet to hear of one such positive outcome.

So that's why taking a time-out is so important. It can prevent you from saying or doing something you really don't want to say or do. Oh, at the moment you might be so upset that you think you want to damage the other, but that's not really what you want to do when you're calm and composed. Calling a time-out can help you avoid inflicting pain that you will likely live to regret.

A time-out signal can take many forms. Some couples use the standard palm over upright fingers gesture that is common at sporting events. I know of one family whose signal is placing their hands on their heads. This tells everyone to "back off because I am about to blow!" One of my favorite time-out signals comes from Bill and Pam Farrel, authors of *Men are Like Waffles, Women are Like Spaghetti*. When they are getting tense and upset with each other, one will state "Hold on. It's not you; it's not me; it's just life. Let's not take it out on each other." Or, "Wait a minute. It's not you; it's not me; we're just both really tired and stressed right now. Let's not do this right now."

A helpful practice my wife and I discovered is that we agree to not discuss sensitive and conflict-filled situations after 9:00pm. We realized that at times when we are both tired and stressed is not the time to take on issues between us. We agree to table whatever the topic is until the next day, when we can approach it with fresh minds and clearer perspectives. You might be thinking about the admonition that you should never go to bed angry. Well, it's a nice thought; however, it could result in very late nights and two people who are already not at their best trying to resolve issues. That's not where I'd place my betting money if you're looking for a pleasant and satisfactory outcome. I can also recall numerous times when I went to bed upset but awoke in the morning wondering why I had been so upset.

I strongly encourage you to adopt a mutually agreed upon time-out signal followed by what you might term a demilitarized zone where combat is strictly forbidden. It is important to remember that this marital skill/practice is **time-out** not **cop out**. By that, I mean that if your spouse has an issue which he or she wants to discuss, you simply must be willing to discuss it at some point. That's one of the responsibilities you took on when you said "I do." If the issue is important to one, then it had better be important to both and must be addressed—just at a time when each can be in a better state from which to discuss calmly and effectively. It is essential that whoever calls for the time-out must schedule the time-in, the time to discuss the matter using the SLT/LUV Talk. The time-in should be within 24 hours, unless you both agree to extend the timeframe.

CHAPTER CHALLENGE

Choose a time-out signal and
get agreement from everyone in
the family to use it to avoid ugly
situations from getting out of hand.
Another of my favorites came from a
couple I helped prepare for marriage.
Their signal was RED—Redirect
Emotional Distress. I took their
suggestion and changed it slightly to
Code Red. You can also combine the
time-in with the time-out by calling
"Code Red, 2:00pm."

*A divorce is like
an amputation;
you survive,
but there's
less of you.*

—Margaret Atwood

SECTION FIVE
PLAY NICE

Never Threaten the Long-Term View

MARRIAGE CAN BE A tricky business. Part of the reason, according to marriage and family expert Dr. Kevin Leman, is that "women are weird and men are strange." While on our good days we can accept and even appreciate the differences between us, on difficult days these differences pose serious threats to the overall health and wellness of the marriage. It's ironic that the differences that can so easily upset us at times are very likely the exact qualities which attracted us to each other in the first place.

You did not marry someone identical to you in all respects—at least if you're smart, you didn't. When you first met your spouse, you were likely attracted—either knowingly or unknowingly—by attributes they possessed that you knew you didn't. You reasoned—again, aware or not—that if you could somehow pair your life with his or hers, you would benefit from his or her strengths. It's not at all a bad concept. While I'm not a big fan of the phrase "you complete me," there is certainly a plus for the relationship when each contributes their unique gifts and strengths to the overall good of the whole.

Given that there are major differences between you and your spouse, it's a tad unrealistic to think there will not be blow-ups and disagreements from time to time in your marriage. So I want to encourage you to adopt a basic rule in your marriage. You and your spouse should agree together that no matter how angry you get, you will never use the "D" word. Scott Stanley, of PREP, and also the University of Denver, says "You should never threaten the long-term view" of the relationship because doing so undermines the motivation of both of you to keep trying and giving your best.

At your wedding, you said "for richer, for poorer, for better or for worse, in sickness and in health, till death do we part"—or words to that effect. You made a vow to each other, and it seems that vows in our modern society no longer mean very much. When in the heat of an argument you threaten to end the marriage, you send shock waves through your partner. He or she begins to question the validity of your initial promise. Talk of divorce or ending the marriage creates an undercurrent of mistrust and each begins to invest less in, but demand more from, the relationship.

Trust me on this—if divorce is a readily available option, it will be chosen far more often than if the parties have decided it is simply not an acceptable choice. Every couple has arguments, and every spouse feels hurt from time to time. You may find this hard to believe, but over our 37+ years together, my wife has gotten upset with me on a few (extremely rare) occasions. Okay, no lightning bolt? I guess I'll keep writing.

Seriously, there have been times in our marriage when we just didn't like each other very much and when each one's negative features seemed to greatly overshadow their positive. If my wife and I considered divorce an option, we might have gone that route rather than doing whatever it took to fix the situation and the relationship.

And fix it we always have. We've always found ways to get back into harmonious love for each other and been glad we didn't cut and run. I know of several other couples who are so glad they made the same decision.

One such couple from my area has become world famous for that very reason. I refer to Kim and Krickitt Carpenter, authors of the *New York Times* bestseller, *The Vow*. Their story was the inspiration for a movie of the same name that has now been shown on movie screens across the country and around the world.

I have to warn you that while the story is true, the dramatic portrayal. . . not so much. You might notice that the movie version went from "based on a true story" to "inspired by a true story" to "inspired by true events." Fortunately, Kim and Krickitt released the updated version of their book on the same day the movie was released.

The subtitle of their book is *"The True Story Behind the Movie,"* and it is indeed a story worth reading of how newlyweds experienced a severe and near tragic accident which could easily have separated them from each other. Fortunately, the Carpenters understood then, as they understand now, the importance of a vow.

It wasn't easy, but with dogged determination and a refusal to quit, they were able to fall back in love with each other and to maintain a successful, joyful, and fulfilling marriage.

Oh, how I wish folks who are planning to marry or those who are in the midst of a troubled marriage would be able to see the big picture and realize that difficulties and challenges and disputes don't need to be the death knell for their marriage. They as individuals, their children, and we as a nation would all benefit if marital vows were given the importance and relevance they were intended to have when they were first made.

While I stand by every word I have written in this book, and in this chapter in particular, I do feel a need to offer a disclaimer. I have at times been accused of believing that people should stay married no matter what. That simply is not accurate. I believe divorce is totally justified in cases of abuse or infidelity—especially when the offensive and hurtful behavior is not going to stop. I'm writing to the vast majority of people who fortunately do not live in those circumstances.

CHAPTER CHALLENGE

Recognize that your marriage
will experience distress,
disappointment, and resentment
from time-to-time. This is normal
and in no way an indication that you
married the wrong person. Covenant
together with your spouse that
no matter how upset you might
be at any given moment, you will
never threaten to end the marriage
or make any suggestion to that
effect. Determine in advance that
you will call a time-out whenever
such words might come out of your
mouth. Review your marriage vows
occasionally to make sure you stay
aware of the commitment you made
to each other.

KIM AND KRICKITT CARPENTER

You just read about the Carpenters, now you get to hear from them in person— well at least technologically speaking.

ProductiveOutcomes.com/ kim-krickitt-carpenter

*Leaving father
and mother's
residence is the
easy part—but
it's not enough.*

—Anonymous

CHAPTER N1
The Number-One Reason Marriages Fail?

ROGER AND JULIE BARRIER have been helping folks succeed in marriage for over 35 years. My wife and I attended a couple's workshop they put on when Roger made the following bold statement: "The number-one reason couples fail in marriage is their failure to leave Mom and Dad."

We've all heard that money is the number-one reason couples struggle and call it quits. I'll not argue that financial mismanagement is a regular source of contention in many marriages. Most couples are stressed at times by children, in-laws, and sexual concerns; and sadly, many couples have ended their marriage without knowing there was help to remedy their situation.

So with all these challenges to marriage, can it really be that the number-one cause of marital breakup is failure to leave one's father and mother? Here it is in Roger's own words: "The degree that Mom and Dad are involved in a marriage is the degree to which they can ruin a marriage. The married couple must be the ones in control of whom they spend time with and how much time they spend." He goes on to say, "Time spent will vary from couple to couple. Seldom is the amount of time the same. It depends on how functional the in-laws are and how well they are able to release control over the children's marriage."

Now please don't get me wrong. I am certainly not suggesting that marriage means you must cut all ties and relationships with your family of origin. That is harmful for other reasons. But there simply must be a balance, and that balance must be determined by the couple, not the in-laws. Drs. Henry Cloud and John Townsend co-authored the bestseller *Boundaries,* in which they give excellent guidance to couples on how to shape and define their lives and their marriage. If you refuse to establish appropriate boundaries, others will do it for you, and I doubt you will like the results.

Failure to leave Mom and Dad often becomes evident when the parents have an inordinate level of influence on decisions the new couple makes. Decisions about where to spend holidays or how to raise the children are just two of many such potential spheres of over-influence.

I certainly believe in the biblical commandment that we are to honor our father and our mother. But honor does not mean that you give them the right to make decisions which are reserved for you and your spouse. Parents should have a place in your marriage, but it must be a subordinate role to that of husband and wife.

A key concept of marriage is that two separate people decide to take on a new identity as a married couple. The formation of this new union, this new "us," must be protected. And while the new relationship might pose an emotional threat to Mom and Dad, they simply must be kept at a safe distance if the new relationship has any chance of thriving.

One very common but dangerous mistake a spouse can make is to run home to his or her parents when having difficulty in their marriage. The smart parents will gently but firmly slam that door in a hurry.

I do heartily advocate that newly married couples find a mature, experienced mentor couple unrelated to either of them. This couple could be an excellent resource in times of strife—especially in the first year when each is trying to figure out the other and their relationship.

The folks at Prepare-Enrich have a network of marriage mentor couples in most, if not every, state in the nation. These couples have been trained to come alongside a couple either preparing for marriage or already married but struggling. They do not have perfect marriages, but they are experienced (each has been married a minimum of five years and most for much longer), and they all have a desire to help others succeed in their marriages.

So if one or both of you feel your parents or in-laws are overly involved in your marriage, let me urge you to have an honest and straightforward talk with them. Please be respectful and grateful for their desire to help. But also be firm that some things need to change.

This would be a wonderful topic to discuss with your marriage mentor couple, who has likely faced the same situation in their marriage. To find such a couple, go to prepare-enrich.com. You and they will be so glad you did.

Please feel free to contact me with any marriage-related questions. I may not know the answer, but I'm confident I will know someone who will.

Oh that we could learn how to communicate well with each other in areas near and dear to our hearts—areas filled with all sorts of emotional content and involvement. When couples can be honest with each other, they can usually reach a mutually acceptable stance on dealing with in-laws and other potentially divisive issues.

CHAPTER CHALLENGE

You know the common phrase from the marriage ceremony "when two are joined together, let no one try to separate them." If you want your marriage to succeed and bring you the joy and intimacy you desire, I suggest you have a respectful conversation with your parents, siblings, or any other "intruders" and let them know how things are going to be different—if that needs to be the case. If others have an overbearing influence on your marriage, you simply must follow Bob Newhart's advice in his classic You Tube video and "Just Stop It!" Consider seeking out a couple you feel has a successful marriage and invite them to share insights with you about how they dealt with or would deal with similar situations.

*A good marriage
at age 50
predicted positive
aging at 80.*

*But, surprisingly,
low cholesterol
levels did not.*

—George Valliant, MD

CHAPTER N2
Beware the Germs that Sicken and Destroy Marriage

I<small>N</small> **2001, I** ATTENDED a three-day pre-conference training institute at my first Smart Marriage Conference. It was titled "The PREP Approach" led by Drs. Howard Markman, Scott Stanley, and Susan Blumberg. These are not likely names well known to you, but they should be.

The PREP Program has now been offered in numerous branches of our military, in most every state, and several foreign countries. It is based on over 30 years of research, mostly conducted at the University of Denver Marriage & Family Studies Department. PREP stands for Prevention and Relationship Education Program. It is designed to "help couples communicate effectively, manage conflict, and nurture fun, friendship, and intimacy in marriage."

One result of those years of research is the book *Fighting for Your Marriage,* in which the authors list "four hallmarks of a great relationship." These hallmarks are:

- Be safe at home.

- Open the doors to intimacy.

- Do your part and be responsible.

- Nurture security in your future together.

Each of these elements would likely make for a worthwhile chapter in their own right, but my focus here is something else that was deeply ingrained in me at that three-day training. Along with these crucial ingredients of a successful marriage, the PREP program covers four common mistakes most couples make that will steal away the joy and contentment they thought they would be getting when they said "I do." The late Dr. Gary Smalley, of the Smalley Relationship Center, took this research and labeled what Markman, Stanley, and Blumberg called Communication Danger Signs, "germs." These germs are found in all types of relationships between coworkers, siblings, spouses, parents and children, neighbors, etc. Once you recognize them, it is much easier to diminish their ability to destroy.

The first germ is Escalation. Escalation occurs when little things quickly become big things. It often sounds like this: "I didn't like it when you did that . . ." followed quickly by:

"Oh, yeah? Well, what about when you did . . ."

The "Oh yeah, oh yeah" cycle continues until you get to a point where whatever you're arguing about has little or nothing to do with whatever started the discussion in the first place. Escalation will occur at some points in every relationship, and it need not be a big deal. If you are in a relationship, however, where escalation occurs frequently and regularly, your relationship is in serious trouble. One or both will likely get to the place where they feel they cannot continue anymore. I'm told that more people leave jobs due to poor relationships with their supervisors than any other cause. I'm willing to wager that Escalation was a recurrent component in their dealings with each other. Escalation is also a common reason why people leave marriages and other relationships.

Before we get to the second germ, let me ask you a question: Perception is reality—true or false? The correct answer is both. If you believe something is true, it is true for you. Your belief, however, no matter how deeply held, does not necessarily make it so. It is well documented that inaccurate perceptions, or what the creators of PREP refer to as Negative Interpretation, can have a very damaging impact on relationships, both at work and at home.

Negative Interpretation occurs when one party ascribes a negative meaning to another's actions, words, thoughts, or motives. You can think of it as being the opposite of giving the benefit of the *doubt* and more giving the benefit of the *blame*. It's thinking the worst of the other. It's believing they are up to no good or somehow out to get you. It's a mess, is what it is, and it's typically unfair, inaccurate, and inappropriate.

I appreciate a quote for which I cannot locate the source: "We judge ourselves by our motives, others by their actions." This does seem to be a very common trait of humans. We know we mess up at times, but we give ourselves credit that we were trying to do the right thing. When others fail, or let us down, our first reaction is to take offense, and not usually to give them credit for having had neutral—or perhaps even good—intentions. We then begin to think of all their negative attributes and how terrible it was for them to purposely treat us that way. Thoughts of revenge often follow. It's a sad truth that Negative Interpretation occurs more often than we might realize.

One major flaw of Negative Interpretation is that we are usually wrong. Dr. J.P. Pawliw-Fry is a recognized expert in the field of Emotional Intelligence. He cites a study which determined adults typically have 60,000 thoughts on any given day. Of these 60,000 thoughts, 95% of them are likely going to be inaccurate or inappropriate. Many will be thoughts about changing the past, which is wasted time and energy because that obviously cannot be done. Or they will be worrisome thoughts about the future, which may or may not ever come to pass. Or they will be guesses about what another person is thinking or what they may have meant by their words or actions. Dr. Pawliw-Fry cautions that such mind reading is an insidious habit which will ruin important relationships in your life.

We simply are not capable of knowing what is going on in the mind of another person. We think we can, however, and then we tend to act on our assumptions, erroneous though they likely are. We experience what researchers call "confirmation bias." Our perceptions become our reality and the driving force in our interactions with others. We begin to see people the way we expect to see them. The other party has been judged guilty without ever knowing they were even accused and are therefore never given a chance for acquittal. I believe most of us would agree we do not appreciate that happening to us. Isn't it time we stop doing it to others?

If you could somehow minimize or eliminate Negative Interpretation from your marriage, you would find yourself having a much more productive and enjoyable relationship.

While all of the germs are powerful and able to destroy a marriage, I personally feel the third—Invalidation—is the worst. Invalidation is the subtle, or not-so-subtle, put-down of another. It is usually, although not always, caustic in nature and is intended to damage another person's character rather than to address the problems, issues, or concerns that occur between you. It can be done by aggressive means or by simply ignoring and disregarding the other's views or interests.

I should note that all of these germs are likely to occur in any relationship—at the workplace, at home, at church—at some time and they are not necessarily lethal to the overall relationship. If allowed to go unchecked, however, they will reach the point where one or both decide to terminate the relationship. Invalidation is one germ which should definitely not occur very often. Words said in anger are usually forgotten quickly by the speaker, but much more slowly, if ever, by the hearer. To attack one's ideas is one thing, but to attack someone personally is an entirely different situation. Each of us knows the sting of hearing degrading comments from someone we thought cared about us and the pain which can linger for years.

It seems to be a shared condition of human beings that we want to be understood. We enjoy being agreed with, but that is secondary to being understood and validated for who we are, what we believe, and how we feel. Because this is what you want, doesn't it make sense that you should strive to give it to others—especially those you live with and encounter on a regular basis? It's not always easy to give respectful validation to another. If you are tired, frustrated, upset, or if the other has come across in an invalidating manner, it can require great effort and discipline to keep your composure and not invalidate the other. But to respond in kind is to engender escalation and worsen rather than improve the situation.

Avoidance/Withdrawal is the fourth of PREP's relationship "germs," which will infect and kill any relationship if given the opportunity to flourish. Avoidance occurs when one or sometimes both parties refuse to address the issues that divide them. They refuse to engage in conversations or situations which are likely to bring up the topic. Withdrawal can be a physical removal of oneself once the conversation has begun. It can also be a mental or emotional disconnection from the conversation. The withdrawer might simply shut down, stop listening, or quickly agree with the other while having no intention to follow through.

Avoidance/Withdrawal causes an ironic, though anything but funny, dance to occur between couples. The norm, it appears, is that in any given disagreement, one person wants to talk and the other doesn't. I call this dance ironic because each party is well motivated, yet they do not appear to be so to the other. The one who wants to discuss, often referred to as the "pursuer," holds the mindset that whatever has come between them can be rectified and does not need to be an ongoing problem in their marriage. Pursuers are typically well motivated, though they do not appear so to the "withdrawer" who is also likely well motivated. Withdrawers often believe that a discussion at that moment is likely to erupt into an unbearable and relationship-harming situation which they wish to avoid.

Therein lies the irony—each spouse is well motivated but appears to be causing trouble. The pursuer, while only wanting to discuss and fix the problem, is left to wonder if the withdrawer is rejecting them or the entire relationship. He or she is then left with no option therefore but to pursue further. This, of course, causes the withdrawer to flee further and faster to avoid the ugliness which he/she is trying to avoid. The withdrawer often gets quite upset, believing the pursuer is only trying to exacerbate an already tense and potentially hostile situation. Each begins to view the other as a threat or enemy, and tensions can easily and quickly escalate out of hand.

John Gottman, Ph.D., Professor Emeritus at the University of Washington, has concluded that the success of a marriage depends not so much on what the differences between the parties may be as it does on how they handle those differences. We humans are so similar in some ways and so tremendously different in others. It is a given that we will disagree with others on occasion. You can admit you sometimes disagree with yourself, so it should come as no surprise that you will often disagree with others. And yet it is a sad fact that most of us have never been trained in how to deal effectively with those differences. We get trained for many tasks we are expected to do in life, yet we ignore addressing the ability to live well together. Certainly these skills should have been developed long before someone enters a marriage, but *should haves* don't take us very far in life or in the home.

Here are some good questions to ask yourself: Is your home a safe place for all inhabitants to share how they truly think? Is it a safe place for them to express their true wants, desires, and preferences? Is it a safe place to bring up concerns? In successful homes, the answers to these questions should always be "yes." If the answers are "no," then Avoidance/Withdrawal is apt to be a frequently occurring problem.

One last "germ" that will sicken and kill off most any relationship is the absence of fun. I learned this from Michelle Weiner-Davis, a superstar in the field of marriage enrichment and restoration. I refer you back to Section One for details about Mrs. Davis and her emphasis that happy, healthy couples simply must make time for fun in their marriage.

I have a hunch that some, if not all, of these germs sound familiar to you. I base this hunch on my experience with hundreds of couples who told me they experience all five in their marriage. Fret not. There are antidotes to these germs and you can be rid of them.

Effective communication is a wonderful antidote for the first four germs. Escalation simply cannot occur if only one person is speaking and the other listening. The same is true for Negative Interpretation as you are checking for accuracy with each paraphrase. You won't be motivated to invalidate your spouse while engaged in a constructive conversation with him or her. And, obviously, if you are speaking with each other, you are not avoiding or withdrawing. I cannot promise you that using the SLT or LUV Talk will ever be what you might consider having fun, but Section One lists ways to address that germ.

My best suggestion for Escalation is to stop it in its tracks. Implement the time-out strategy and postpone the conversation until a more convenient and productive time.

So what are you to do if Negative Interpretation is impacting your relationship? If you suspect you are on the receiving end, you should look for an opportunity to **gently and directly** confront the other and ask if it might be occurring. Ask, without accusing, if they have an issue with something you may have said or done. Be prepared for a quick denial and change of subject. A second visit may be required to get to the heart of the matter.

If you realize you may have regarded your spouse in a negative light, begin to challenge your thoughts about him or her. Is he or she really as terrible as your thoughts about them have led you to believe? Instead of giving the benefit of the blame, why not practice AGI, which I describe in Chapter 3 of *PLAY NICE in Your Sandbox at Work*. The chapter is available at PlayNiceinYourSandbox.com. Force yourself if necessary to consider what might be a reasonable and appropriate underlying motive for the other's actions or words.

As I said previously, I believe that Invalidation is the worst of the germs and the best remedy is to avoid it at all costs. Take a time-out, get a grip on your emotions, and make rational decisions. Try to stay in the thinking portion of your brain rather than giving full vent to your emotional or limbic area. As the late Dr. Stephen Covey advised, choose to respond, rather than simply react to a perceived slight.

If the Invalidation has already occurred, apologize as quickly and as sincerely as you are able. Give the person some time to accept your apology and be prepared to have to offer another, depending on the depth of pain you inflicted.

If you are on the receiving end of Invalidation, my best advice is to forgive and move on. Often more easily said than done, I admit, but I can see no better alternative. Refer back to Chapter A2 to review thoughts on how to do this well.

It seems we have become such a fragile society where every little offense is magnified and blown way out of proportion, and unfortunately home is no exception. For sure, some relationships have been damaged far beyond the point of repair. But many relationships could be greatly improved if we could learn to take ourselves a little less seriously and give more validation to others. Trust me, you will daily encounter folks who are so hungry for a little validation—this is perhaps doubly true for those living in your household.

Although every marriage will experience the five germs at times, with proper prevention and remediation, they need not be fatal to the relationship.

CHAPTER CHALLENGE

Read this chapter again with your spouse and discuss which of the five germs are most prevalent or most damaging in your relationship. Choose one and determine to vaccinate yourselves from it over the next 30 days. Purchase a copy of *Fighting for Your Marriage* and commit to reading a chapter together each week.

There is also a deeply thought through Christian version of this topic by Scott Stanley and colleagues, presented in a book called *A Lasting Promise* (2014). They have developed various materials that can be used with Christians in workshops and home studies, also under the title of A Lasting Promise. See alastingpromise.com for more details.

For every minute you remain angry, you give up sixty seconds of peace of mind.

—Ralph Waldo Emerson

CHAPTER **N3**
The G.I.F.T. of Anger?

WHEN SOMEONE YOU CONNECT with is hurting, they will likely let you know in less-than-positive ways. You then have a choice to make. You can either react to the anger and watch the rest of your day go downhill, or you can choose to attempt to help ease their pain and avoid causing further grief.

You don't have to take it personally when someone "goes off" on you. I mean that—you don't *have to* take it personally. The fact that most of us do in no way undermines the truth of what you just read. While you are the recipient of someone's displeasure at the moment, it quite possibly has little or nothing to do with you. If you take it personally and get defensive, you will miss out on an opportunity to help them deal with whatever is bothering him or her. And once that opportunity is gone, it may not come back for quite some time.

There are many possible reasons for why your spouse or child is attacking you or taking out their frustration on you. Anger is a secondary emotion. We are never angry just because we are angry. Drs. Tom and Beverly Rodgers of the Rodgers Christian Counseling Center in Charlotte, NC cite four major reasons why people get angry.

The first is *guilt*. If you are feeling guilty about something, it is only a matter of time before you quit berating yourself and turn your anger outward.

The second underlying cause of anger is actually two, but both start with the letter *I*. If you are feeling *inferior* to someone, it can easily set you off and lead to anger. The same is true if you are feeling *inadequate* to meet the demands of a task.

Fear is the third reason you might resort to anger.

The fourth component is *trauma*, or what the Rodgers refer to as reliving a painful memory from your past. You, like all the rest of us, were probably wounded in some ways when you were young and a spontaneous memory of those painful times can blindside you at any moment, causing you to get angry.

The first letters of these terms (using just one of the *I*'s) spell out the word GIFT. Anger then may be viewed as a gift telling you that something is not quite right. The Rodgers recommend that whenever you feel angry, you should grab your thumb, look at your fingers, and ask yourself which of these factors may be causing your anger. If you can figure out the cause, you have a far greater chance of determining an appropriate response and course of action.

I have a vivid memory of an opportunity I had to practice the "grab your thumb" technique. Several years ago, I was tossing and turning in bed; sleep was not happening. My restlessness indicated how upset I was with my wife, who was in another room, blissfully unaware of my agitated state. After a time, I decided I would walk down the hall and give her a piece of my mind (though it's not like I have that many extra pieces to spare).

I threw the covers off, jumped out of bed and stormed—not walked—stormed down the hall. About halfway down, I paused and grabbed my thumb and asked myself if I was angry. "Yes, I'm ANGRY!" was my reply. I then asked myself what I should do about my anger. While I did not have a direct answer right away, I did realize what I *should not* do—barge in and unload on my wife.

To be honest, I cannot remember what happened next. I'm confident it was one of two scenarios. Either I calmly walked over to her and asked if we could talk, (using the LUV Talk) or I turned around and went back to bed, thereby postponing the conversation until the next day. While I cannot remember what I did, I am certain I would well remember the episode if I had indeed ripped into her.

I'll leave you with one other technique to help avoid anger getting the best of you. The next time you find yourself in an agitated state carefully monitor your self-talk. If you hear yourself using the pronoun "I" or "me" quickly replace that with "you." Rather than focusing on how upset **I** am or how dare they do that to **me**, try making internal statements like "you're pretty upset right now" or "you sure took offense at that remark."

By talking to yourself in the second person you literally help to transition out of your emotional brain and into your thinking brain, from which you are far more likely to make a reasoned and appropriate response. I find it even more helpful to talk to myself in the third person by using my first name as in "Ron, you sure are upset at the moment. Ron, what do you think you should do right now?"

I can't give you all the scientific reasons for why this works so effectively, but I can assure you it works well in most, if not all, situations.

Anger is so common and so destructive in the home, we'll look more at how you can prevent it from occurring in the next chapter.

CHAPTER CHALLENGE

Discuss with your spouse and children the concept of grabbing your thumb, or speaking to yourself in the 2nd or 3rd person to gain control over emotions. Encourage all to form the habit and refuse to put up with tantrums from any— regardless their age, or position in the household. I wrote more about the Grab Your Thumb technique in PLAY NICE in Your Sandbox at Work, and while I again encourage you to purchase a copy for yourself, I have posted the chapter at my website: PlayNiceinYourSandbox.com.

TOM AND BEV RODGERS

If your knee hurts or your tooth aches, you're eventually going to see a professional who can provide some relief. Well why not do the same if your marriage is hurting? In this short video clip Drs. Tom and Beverly Rodgers talk about a program they offer that has great results in transforming deeply troubled marriages into ones that thrive.

**ProductiveOutcomes.com/
drs-tom-beverly-rodgers**

*It's not wise
to violate rules
until you
know how to
observe them.*

—**T. S. Eliot**

CHAPTER N4
Could These Ground Rules Keep You from Flying Off the Handle?

I KNOW YOU THINK YOU heard what I said, but I'm not certain you realize that what I said is not really what I think you thought I meant. *Say what?* Most miscommunications in marriage aren't quite that far off and certainly not so humorous. The odds are high that you know of a couple, or perhaps several couples, who have split up because they didn't know how to communicate well together. It seems they can communicate just fine with others—but not with each other.

One common reason couples have difficulty communicating well together is it doesn't feel safe for them to do so. If one or the other feels the communication might go south and have a negative result, he or she is not likely going to be too excited about entering into the conversation. The Speaker–Listener Technique that I shared in a previous chapter can help to create safety within a conversation. Here are a few more suggestions for you to consider.

Some years ago, I attended a workshop given by Tom Strohl, where he detailed what he termed "Four Ground Rules for Safety." The first such ground rule is "No Zingers." If you've known your spouse for any substantial period, you are likely quite skilled at being able to push his or her buttons. You likely know just the right words or phrases that can send them into anger faster than a speeding bullet and be more powerful than a locomotive. Well, just because you *can* do something doesn't necessarily mean you *should* do it. And if you want meaningful communication with your spouse, you surely will want to refrain from sending verbal jabs in his or her direction.

Certainly, you will get frustrated with your spouse at times, and it's so easy at those times to let him or her know how frustrated you are. The problem is that while eventually you will calm down, the damage caused by your hurtful words can take a long time to dissipate. It is far better to avoid causing the damage than it is to try to fix it later. You can't unring a bell, and you can't take back hurtful words— at least not easily or quickly.

Tom realized that while adopting the rule of "No Zingers" was helpful, it might not always be practical in the heat of a battle. This explains the importance of Rule

Number Two: Time-Out. (I wrote about the importance of calling a time-out in Chapter Y3, but feel it is well worth repeating here.) By adopting this second rule, the couple agreed that if they ever got to a place where they were so upset, so hurt, or so angry that they wanted to hurt the other, they would first call a time-out. I have found time-out to be a hugely effective tool for resolving disputes as it can mitigate further damage to an already-heated situation.

You tend to think primarily with one part of your brain (the frontal lobe), and you feel mostly with another (the limbic system). There are times when you can get so into your feeling brain that you literally stop thinking. That helps to explain (but not excuse) road rage. It also helps to explain relationship rage, and it simply must not be allowed to occur. I encourage you to come up with a time-out signal that every member of the family clearly understands and that indicates the discussion must abruptly stop and be rescheduled at a later time.

This rescheduling is also a vital piece of the rule. We're talking time-out, not copout. Therefore whoever calls for the time-out is obligated to call the time-in, a time when he or she will be back in their thinking brain and willing to discuss the issue that caused the upheaval in the first place. That way your spouse is not left wondering whether you are rejecting him or her, the relationship, or simply the argument—which is often the case.

Time-outs typically should be no less than 30 minutes to give your body a chance to calm down, and no longer than 24 hours, so the other party knows that his or her concerns will be addressed. You could call for a short time-out and discuss the situation using the Speaker-Listener-Technique, or LUV talk, which we addressed in Chapter Y2.

Sometimes, you just need to acknowledge that you both got a little sideways and there may not be something more to talk about. Other times, when what sparked the conflict was an important issue or problem, you especially need to make that time to talk about it in a better way.

Rule Number Three of Mr. Strohl's four is "No Punishment." I must remind you that these rules are intended to help protect and maintain your marriage. If that is not your desire, then, by all means, attack away with everything you've got. Just be sure you're prepared for the likely outcome of a severed and perhaps irreparably damaged relationship. If, however, you want the relationship to continue and improve, then refraining from exacting a pound of flesh or any sort of revenge/punishment is likely the better way to go.

It's one thing to be upset with your spouse; it's something entirely different to want him or her to have to pay for what they did. Trust me, it's difficult to keep a happy marriage and want retribution at the same time. You really must decide which is more important to you.

The fourth and final Ground Rule for Safety is "Talk by Agreement." This is related to the "Time-Out" rule in that both parties agree to a) when and where they should meet and b) what they should talk about. In this way, neither feels put upon or pressured as each has consented to the conversation. Ideally, the spouses will also agree to use the Speaker–Listener Technique to ensure the conversation is productive and cordial.

You can look back over your marriage and recognize times when you wanted to talk but your spouse didn't. The reverse is also likely true that there have been times when your spouse wanted to talk, but you didn't. That's why Rule

Number Four is so important, that you agree that you will only discuss sensitive issues when you both agree you are in a proper frame of mind and heart to do so.

Are these four ground rules guaranteed to fix any and all marital problems? Of course not! But what they can do is help each person feel safe in the relationship. Each should be more willing to fix what's broken if they know they will not be attacked, that they can escape the conflict with a time-out, that they will not be punished, and that they will only have to talk when they are prepared to do so. I can attest that these ground rules are helpful in a marriage-coaching session. I invite you to consider how valuable they may be in your home.

CHAPTER CHALLENGE

Consider writing these four ground rules in calligraphy, or some special font, and post them in a conspicuous place in your house. This will serve to remind you to put them into practice. It could also be a help to visitors in your home, who likely are not aware of them but need to be.

Unless both sides win, no agreement can be permanent.

—Jimmy Carter

SECTION SIX
PLAY NICE

Insist on Win-Win:
A recipe for growth and prosperity

I OFTEN SAY THAT "PEOPLE who think they know it all are awfully annoying to those of us who really do." No one who knows me well would ever say I think I know it all, for I am a habitual training junkie. I am ever on the lookout for a workshop, book, course or other means to increase my knowledge and ability to do life well.

Several years ago, I attended a keynote given by Eileen McDargh, where she gave an illustration I have used numerous times in my work with couples. She told of two people in a rowboat that developed a leak near the front.

The person nearest the front spotted the problem and immediately went to work bailing like crazy. The person in the back spotted the problem, but rather than joining the relief effort, stood back and stated, "I'm glad that hole is not on *my* side of the boat."

Perhaps you have heard the expression "We're all in the same boat." No place should this be truer than in marriage and family relationships. My friend and colleague Richard Marks is big on the concept of "us" in marriage. He asserts that unless both parties win, no one wins.

Dr. Robert Paul with the National Institute of Marriage tells a story of how this concept also relates to parenting. He and his son—I believe his son was ten at the time—had a disagreement, which Dr. Paul thought he needed to address. Following a private conversation, he felt the matter was resolved to each one's satisfaction. His son's dejected mood at the dinner table told him otherwise. Mr. Paul asked his son who he thought won in the conversation they had before dinner. Taken aback by the question, the son asked him what he meant. Dr. Paul repeated the question—in their conversation, who came out victorious, to which the son replied, "You did, Dad."

After stating that he disagreed, Dr. Paul asked him if he could imagine a baseball game that he might win and his close friend Chucky (I made up the name as I can't remember for sure) might lose? "No," his son adamantly replied. Dr. Paul then asked if he could foresee a game that Chucky might win and he lose, which again resulted in an impassioned "No!"

"Why not?" Dr. Paul asked.

"Because we're on the same team, Dad" was the somewhat irritated reply. Dr. Paul calmly but firmly assured his son that he felt he and his son were also on the same team and if the son did not feel he was a co-winner, then the matter must be addressed again until they reached a win-win resolution.

Conflict has a negative connotation for many, yet conflict in the home is inevitable. You simply cannot put two or more imperfect people in continuous proximity to each other and not expect there to be disagreements from time-to-time. While it is true that when conflict is not handled well, relationships can be severely damaged, it is also true that conflict has positive attributes. According to William Ellery Channing "Difficulties are meant to rouse, not discourage. The human spirit is to grow strong by conflict."

Competition has its place in our culture, but aside from playful games or activities, competition is never appropriate in a marriage or a family. If you and your spouse are truly united, then where is the satisfaction of triumph or conquest? Instead of trying to win over your life partner, why not rather try to win your life partner over?

Think Win-Win is Habit Four in Dr. Stephen Covey's *The Seven Habits of Highly Effective People*. He expands on the theme by adding "or no deal for now." Such thinking leaves the door open to the fact that while no mutually agreeable resolution may come to you at the moment, such a resolution might become apparent at a later time. I'm not saying this will always be easy, but I'm confident it will always be your best option.

CHAPTER CHALLENGE

When faced with a seemingly unsolvable challenge, insist on viewing the issue from an "us" perspective and don't stop seeking until both are content with the outcome. By the way, I strongly recommend you adhere to the traditional definition of win-win, not the humorous version I heard, which defines win-win as "Do it my way, and nobody gets hurt."

DR. BOB PAUL

There are many factors which can prevent a couple from engaging in win-win behavior. As you about to hear, fear is often a present factor.

**ProductiveOutcomes.com/
dr-bob-paul**

In many instances, marriage vows would be more accurate if the phrase were changed to "Until debt do us part."

—Sam Ewing

CHAPTER 11
Money is a Fact of Life

I F I WERE TO ask you to tell me the four main reasons couples divorce today, you would likely tell me money, sex, children, and in-laws. You would be in the majority with that response, but you would still be incorrect.

Money, sex, children, and in-laws are challenges most every married couple has to face. It's how they face them that determines the overall health and success of their marriage. It might be helpful to address each of these challenges, however, to provide some useful tips to better navigate your way through them.

The first point I want to make is that money does not make or break a marriage. We have all heard stories of very wealthy couples who had miserable marriages, and seemingly worse divorces. Their divorce attorneys rejoiced, but few others did. You have likely known couples who had very little regarding this world's riches but had a deep and abiding love for, and commitment to, each other. You also know couples of great means and wealth who have the same degree of marital happiness, so how well a couple will do in their marriage simply can't be a matter of how much or how little money they have.

The fact remains that many couples often argue over money and finances. I believe there are many reasons for this. One reason, of course, could be old-fashioned control. One or both might feel a need to control the other, and deciding how the money will or will not be spent is a convenient way to exercise that control. So while the argument will be over money, the real cause for the dissension is control.

Another reason couples fight over money could be a matter of security. It is not a matter of right or wrong, or of better or worse, but some of us have a strong desire—make that need—to have financial security. If this is a driving force for one but not the other, money is bound to be the focus of arguments. But, again, the matter is not money but security.

You have heard the expression that "opposites attract," and there is absolute truth in that statement. You and your spouse are likely very different in many key areas of life, so it should come as no surprise that money just might be one of those areas of difference. Much of the challenge in marriage, especially in the early years, is figuring out how to blend those differences into a new identity as a married couple.

If you care little about money and enjoy giving it away, you may have married someone who sees the accumulation of wealth as a status to be attained or a pathway to happiness. If you are one of those security-conscious folks I mentioned above, the chances are good that your life partner is far more carefree.

While the challenge of merging divergent personalities and life preferences may seem daunting at times, please consider the opposite for a moment. Consider what life would be like if you married someone who was your clone, an exact representation of you. I don't know about you, but that thought sends shivers up my spine.

So, as the French say, "Vive la différence!" Having said that, wouldn't it be nice if you could truly identify the real issues in your arguments over money? Wouldn't it be nice if you could come together over spending, budgeting, and getting out of debt? Wouldn't it be nice if you were on the same team regarding building, maintaining, or repairing credit? How about if you could learn and understand your partner's attitudes and habits with money?

Well, I have good news for you. All these concerns can be dealt with successfully, so they are not continuous thorns in your proverbial marital side. You are going to have to learn some new things if you're ever going to get to that place, but you will not have to figure it out on your own. Help and guidance are widely available in our society to empower couples to get a handle on their finances. Here are two such resources, one is fairly well known, the other not so much.

The well-known resource is Financial Peace University created and led by the shy and timid Dave Ramsey. Okay, maybe I'm off on the shy and timid part, but trust me this is a program well worth the time, effort, and money it requires. Mr. Ramsey has gained fame with his straight-shooting, no-nonsense approach to life and finances. Couples who complete his course have a solid footing on which to build their financial lives together. As with any advice, you must determine the applicability and appropriateness to your particular situation.

An excellent resource you likely have not heard of is Money Habitudes, created by Syble Solomon. Money Habitudes is a card game designed to help couples understand and appreciate each other's habits and attitudes regarding the financial aspect of their marriage. By playing this card game, couples can discuss their differences in a non-threatening, respectful and loving manner. That might not be as exciting as fighting, but I'll let you decide which is preferable.

CHAPTER CHALLENGE

At the risk of sounding like a broken record: set aside some time to discuss your thoughts and concerns about money. Since you know this will likely be a sensitive topic, be sure to use the LUV Talk. Do a web search to see if there is a Financial Peace University course in your area and consider purchasing a set of Money Habitudes cards.

SYBLE SOLOMON

I could say more about Money Habitudes and how it can be an asset in your marriage, but I thought you should hear about it from the inventor herself.

**ProductiveOutcomes.com/
syble-solomon**

I'm certain that most couples expect to find intimacy in marriage, but it somehow eludes them.

—Dr. James Dobson

CHAPTER 12
Sex is a Fact of Married Life

A S I MENTIONED IN the previous chapter, while there are always exceptions to any rule, it is a basic fact of marriage that opposites attract. If you're a planner, you likely married a free spirit. If you are a stern disciplinarian, you likely married someone with more parental tolerance. If you have a close relationship with your family of origin, you likely married someone who is somewhat estranged from their family. While it is certainly not a hard-and-fast rule that you are opposites in these three areas, I'm willing to bet you are in the area of sex.

That, by the way, is based on the fact that men and women are so different from each other in how they view and feel about this very important area of marriage. Let me first point out, however, that great sex does not necessarily make for a great marriage, but a great marriage does usually lead to great sex.

One fundamental way in which men and women differ over sex is in how often they think about it. According to Dr. Kevin Leman, author of *Turn up the Heat*, *Sheet Music*, and some 40 other marriage and family books, men think about sex 33 times as often as women. In his words, "Men think about sex all day long." Now ladies, before you attach the pervert label to all men, may I please take a moment to mention the "T" word?

The "T" word is testosterone. Testosterone is the primary sex hormone in men, and while it is also found in women, his levels are typically much, much higher than hers. Dr. Pat Love, a professor, counselor/therapist, and Certified Love Educator, is the author of *How to Improve Your Marriage Without Talking About It*, *Hot Monogamy*, and *The Truth About Love*.

I mention Dr. Love because I heard her state that she had always been curious about testosterone and wanted to find out for herself what it was all about. She related that she met with a medical doctor, who injected her with a male's dosage of the hormone. She said that within 20 minutes, she began staring at men's crotches, fantasizing about sex, and had an irresistible urge to rush home and drag her husband into the bedroom. She said emphatically that she now realized how dangerous this stuff was and how quickly she wanted to get off it.

Welcome, ladies, to the life of your man. This is a battle which men must fight continuously throughout the day. Men are also visually stimulated, which makes summertime extremely challenging, if you get my drift.

Now men, please note I am in no way giving you permission to act on your sexual urges and like Flip Wilson of olden days say, "The testosterone made me do it!" Stephen Arterburn, Fred Stoeker, and Mike Yorkey wrote a classic book, *Every Man's Battle: Every Man's Guide to Winning the War on Sexual Temptation One Victory at a Time*. They provide great insight and guidance into how best to manage and control the urges that testosterone produces, but which simply must be overcome in all situations outside of the marital bedroom. I highly recommend that every man, and every woman for that matter, read *Every Man's Battle*.

Another significant difference between the genders is that one is often well satisfied with having sex, while the other is typically only interested in lovemaking—and there is a huge difference between the two. Again quoting Dr. Leman, "Men only need a place, but women need a reason." He goes on to say that "as a husband and wife understand and learn to appreciate those crucial differences, they can turn up the heat in their relationship and have great sex—all the time."

Men need to realize that for many women, engaging in sex and/or lovemaking requires energy that the typical woman cannot just turn on as easily as he can. For most women, the act of sex is a meaningful emotional process, not just a physically indulgent event.

The bottom line of what I'm trying to say is that this vital area of marriage must be discussed and better understood by both parties. Unfortunately, these conversations are not common or regular in most marriages. Dr. Leman states, "Most couples spend one percent of their sexual relationship talking about it and 99 percent making love." Let me please encourage you to balance out that equation a bit better. You might want to get a copy of Dr. Leman's books *Turn Up the Heat* and *Sheet Music* for some excellent guidance and worthwhile advice. It seems there is such shame and stigma attached to sex and yet it need not and should not be that way.

I had no illusions that I would cover all that should be said about marital sex in this chapter, but I do hope I have spurred an interest for you to make this a topic of conversation in hopes of coming to some mutually agreeable and satisfying decisions.

CHAPTER CHALLENGE

Be willing to admit you may not know everything you need to know about how to fulfill your spouse's sexual needs. Invite him or her to tell you what he or she would appreciate receiving from you, and tell them what you prefer or desire. Be respectful and do not ask your spouse to do something that is totally against what he or she is willing to do. Please remember, it's about intimacy and connection far more than physical pleasure.

Parents need to fill a child's bucket of self-esteem so high that the rest of the world can't poke enough holes to drain it dry.

—Alvin Price

CHAPTER 13
Parenting is a Team Sport

HERE COMES A CHAPTER on parenting from someone who has never made an error in parenting judgment. I have never said a wrong word, done a wrong deed, or even thought a wrong thought when it comes to parenting my children. Now that should tell you one of three things about me: I'm a fool, I'm a liar, or I have no children. I guess all three might be possible, but my preferred answer is that I have no children. I never have, and seriously doubt I ever will.

That being said, I do want to share some thoughts on the impact of children on a marriage. For starters, let me say that if your marriage is in trouble, having a child, or another child is likely not the best prescription for improvement. Many couples have gone that route, and many of them have later come to me for divorce mediation. Children can certainly bring a couple closer to each other, but usually not as a solution to their marital problems.

Another very common parenting mistake I have observed over my career as a mediator and marriage coach is that spouses neglect their marriage for the sake of the children. I wish I had counted all the times I've heard divorcing parents tell me they chose to put their children first and failed to focus on their marriage. While very common, that's about the most convoluted logic I've ever heard. If you want to put your children first, then give them what they want and need most—two parents who love and respect each other and who provide for them a safe, happy environment from which to launch into adulthood.

All parents should have the names of capable, qualified childcare providers, and they should utilize them on a regular basis. Sure, your children will complain that they want to go with you, but they will thank you years later for spending quality and quantity time together as a couple.

Many parents make the mistake of expecting perfection in their parenting. Sorry to break the news to you, but that is an absolutely unrealistic and potentially harmful expectation to put on yourself or your spouse. When it comes to parenting, perfection is just not going to happen. The main reason for this is that all parties—parents and children— are less than perfect. The only reason I mention this fairly obvious thought is that most parents set out to be perfect. How often did you swear you would do a better job than your parents and later found yourself acting or sounding just like they did?

It's also true that most parents have a deep-seated fear that they are somehow going to mess up and scar their child(ren) for life. In most cases, this is a totally irrational fear, but its power and influence are not tied to its truthfulness or lack thereof. Please note, however, that if your spouse already has this fear button in place and you decide to push it with a critical comment, you might want to wear a flak jacket or have a good running head start when you do.

Parenting is a matter which thrives in an atmosphere of mutual respect and open communication. It is also a skill which typically requires some refinement and acquired knowledge. Parenting experts and materials abound in our society. Some of my personal favorites are James Dobson, Kevin Leman, John Rosemond, and Foster Cline, Charles Fay and Jim Fay (of *Love and Logic* fame). For step-parenting, there is probably none better than Ron Deal. I really like Robert Lewis for helping fathers help their adolescent son's transition to manhood.

Let me close with a word about spanking. In my humble opinion, spanking is the absolute worst form of punishment known to man. For a child to be severely struck by the person or persons who are supposed to be their caregivers is tantamount to inhumane treatment and outright cruelty. Having said that, however, I firmly believe that spanking done properly is—at the appropriate ages—the best form of discipline known to man. Please note there is a huge difference between *punishment* and *discipline*. The former is for the sake of the giver and spanking becomes an opportunity to release anger and to vent rage on the recipient. That is never acceptable.

Discipline, however, is for the sake of the receiver and has a much different purpose. Loving, controlled spanking as discipline is designed to help the child learn valuable life lessons and need never be harsh or severe. It should also never be meted out in anger. I suggest that spanking must be a three-step process. It begins with making sure the child knows what he or she did wrong that merits corrective measures. (That's just one more reason why infants should never be spanked. All they will learn is that you have the power to hurt them and that you're not afraid to use that power.)

The second step in spanking as discipline is the administration of mild to moderate, controlled force on the well-padded bottom—never in the face. Again, it is not the force which delivers the message—unless the force is excessive, which sends the wrong message.

The third step in spanking as discipline is the loving, reassuring embrace you give to your child. This helps him or her realize they have been corrected because of their behavior and not because they are an awful person. These hugs can be special times when the child grows to appreciate the loving concern demonstrated by the parent, and should never be omitted.

So much more could be said about other parenting issues, such as spending quality and quantity time with your children. I'm reminded of the father who asked his son if he wanted quality time or quantity time. The son replied, "I want quality time Dad, and lots of it!" Your children need to know they matter to you.

We could talk about the importance of spending one-on-one time with each child, and other matters, but that is not my focus in this book. I simply want to encourage you to make sure you and your spouse are talking about your parenting in a cooperative "we're in this together" tone. If you do this, and if you'll do whatever you need to do to learn how to do it well, both your parenting and your marriage will prosper.

CHAPTER CHALLENGE

Review the list of parenting experts I cited in this chapter. Do some research online and choose one to model your parenting on. You likely have friends you consider to be excellent parents. Be brave and ask them for advice, or for resources they have found to be valuable.

RON DEAL

Since so many in our society face the enormous challenge of step-parenting, I thought you might know someone who would appreciate some expert advice on the subject. I'm not the one to provide that for you but Ron Deal is. Click on the code and see for yourself.

ProductiveOutcomes.com/ ron-deal

*Great things
are not done by
impulse, but by
a series of small
things brought
together.*
—George Eliot

CHAPTER 14
Marriage as a Business?

THERE ARE TWO TIMES each year when most of us take stock of our lives and determine what changes might be necessary or beneficial. The first is our annual trip around the sun on our birthday. The second, obviously, is the beginning of each new year. This is a season when hope springs eternal, and we set out to be the man or woman we truly want to be. I've decided I want to be the person my dog thinks I am—but that's a different story.

So as you near either of these yearly milestones, I invite you to look back for a bit and determine how you did in your marriage over the previous 365 days. Did you function well as a team? Did you grow together as individuals and as a couple? Did you accomplish the goals you set for your marriage at the beginning of the year? That is, of course, if you set goals in the first place.

I believe the practice of reviewing the past year has merit, but I am convinced that looking forward to the next is potentially even more beneficial. You have an opportunity to take a few moments and gain some direction and purpose for your relationship. I highly recommend the book *The 12 Week Year* by Brian P. Moran and Michael Lennington. The authors suggest that year-long planning is a flawed way to manage one's career, relationships, and life. Twelve months is a long time to forecast, especially with the fast-changing pace of life. They suggest instead that you look forward 12 weeks and set reasonable objectives you want to accomplish during that period.

The end of the each year is a wonderful time for couples to sit down and discuss their relationship. You could determine the state of your union, so-to-speak. Far too many couples have no goals or objectives they want to achieve as a couple. They may have individual goals, but couples' goals are often lacking. Of course planning your marriage can occur at any time of the year. The "what" is more important than the "when."

So am I suggesting that your marriage should resemble a business? If I did, I certainly would not be the first to do so. Dr. John Curtis is the author of *The Business of Love*. In his book and companion workbook, Dr. Curtis shows you how to apply "proven business strategies to 'divorce-proof'" your marriage. He details the importance of vision planning, regular staff meetings, setting budgets, etc. as being essential to the overall well-being of a business. He goes on to say the same for a marriage. Many fail at marriage, due in part to the absence of intentional planning and direction.

As found on his website drjohncurtis.com, information in *The Business of Love* will help couples to:

- Develop measurable objectives that define why the relationship exists, where it is headed, and how you will measure success.

- Determine attitudes about money and those attitudes' roles in successfully funding the marital enterprise.

- Develop a relationship "love logo" and market a unified "relationship brand."

- Learn how to deal with the consequences of "mergers and acquisitions" in the context of couples, blended families, and children from other relationships.

- Create job descriptions and stop bickering about who does what around the house.

- Design a relationship-feedback process complete with tips on regular appraisal sessions.

The main point I take from Dr. Curtis's work is that he gives couples structure upon which they can build an intentional marriage. I've written several times over the years that intentionality is a powerful component of successful marriage.

Perhaps thinking of your marriage as a business is not to your liking, so let me suggest another option. Clint and Penny Bragg, of Inverse Ministries, have developed a concept they call Mini-Marriage Retreats (MMRs). For several years, they have set aside time every 90 days to get away and strategize what they want to accomplish in the next 90 days. In their words, "The concept behind the MMR is simple: every ninety days, we get away to assess and set marriage goals in seven different areas: Spiritual, Relationships, Finances, Professional, Health, Home, and Big Dreams."

They pick a location near their home, but far enough away to minimize the temptation to end their planning time too soon, and they go there for all or part of a weekend. Typically they select a reasonably priced hotel, and after checking in, they go out for a nice evening together. The next day is set aside for their Retreat session. They review their objectives from their previous MMR and rate how well they did in achieving their objectives. They then look forward and plan their next 90 days. Objectives from the previous session may or may not be carried over, depending on their current state of importance.

You can learn more about Mini Marriage Retreats in the Bragg's book, *Marriage on the Mend—Healing Your Relationship After Crisis, Separation, or Divorce* or at their website inverseministries.org.

Is all this planning and thinking about marriage necessary? No, but there are a lot of divorced folks who wish now that they had done so while they were still married. Successful marriage typically does not happen by circumstance. It need not require 24/7/365 focus, but some attention is certainly advisable.

CHAPTER CHALLENGE

Visit the websites cited in this chapter and gather more information about becoming more strategic in your marriage. Get your calendars and plan times to put these recommended programs into action.

DR. JOHN CURTIS

In this brief video Dr. Curtis and I visit about one particular aspect of marriage you and your spouse have likely never considered. Watch and decide if maybe you should?

**ProductiveOutcomes.com/
dr-john-curtis**

Commitment is making a choice to give up other choices.

—Dr. Scott Stanley

SECTION SEVEN
PLAY NICE

Commitment:
A matter of life or death?

A HUSBAND AND WIFE WERE having an argument when the husband blurted out, "I was a fool when I married you." The wife maintained her composure and calmly replied: "I suppose you were, dear, but at the time I was so much in love, I didn't even notice." At the risk of sounding like a broken record, married couples will experience times in their marriage when they don't especially like each other. This shouldn't come as a great surprise as there are times in most of our lives that we don't like ourselves all that much. We let ourselves or others down and beat ourselves up for it. If that is true, that we are not always comfortable with our own behavior, what chance is there that we will always be totally comfortable with someone else? And therein lies the great need for commitment if your marriage is to be all that you hoped for when you first said, "I do."

Commitment appears to be a vanishing quality in our society. When something isn't working just right, we replace it with a newer, more up-to-date version. This is fine if you're talking about a mattress or television set. It's not so good if you're talking about a marriage partner. My fear is that we have not prepared folks for the reality that any marriage will have challenging moments. Anyone who has been married more than five years and tells you the thought of divorce has never entered their minds will likely lie to you about other things as well. Or if not divorce, they have at least entertained thoughts that maybe they married the wrong person or that getting married was a mistake. That is normal, and those thoughts need to be taken to the recycle bin in your mind and quickly deleted.

Another problem I see is that many folks have a lowered concept of what marriage can be and therefore settle for less. They also hesitate to fully invest in the marriage for fear the payout will not be worth the investment. Dr. Scott Stanley, who I have cited a few times previously, has authored or co-authored numerous books and journal articles and has participated in several studies designed to find out why marriages fail and how to help them succeed. In his book, *The Power of Commitment*, Dr. Stanley writes that "only in the context of a total commitment are you free to develop greater levels of intimacy and connection—the things that are perhaps the very essence of oneness." What a paradox. We want true and lasting commitment, but we're afraid to give it ourselves for fear it will not be reciprocated.

Dr. Stanley describes two forms of commitment, each of which is vital to a lasting, satisfying marriage. One is dedication commitment, which "implies an internal state of devotion to a person or project." This is the fun part of commitment. It's the part where you want to be with your spouse because you are being fulfilled and feel like you are adding value to his or her life as well. Every marriage needs a healthy dose of dedication commitment to be successful and high functioning.

The second form of commitment is what Dr. Stanley calls constraint commitment which "brings out the sense of obligation." You may not be very happy with the state of your marriage, but the cost of divorce, the impact on the children, and the grief you will cause family and friends serves as a deterrent to ending the marriage. As with dedication commitment, every couple needs constraint commitment from time to time. When things get rough, as they will, you need to buckle down and fix what's broken. Cutting and running should rarely be an option at all and certainly never the first option. When divorce is a readily available option, folks are more likely to choose it than to do what's necessary to make things better.

I'm reminded of the Biosphere, a failed experiment of controlled living in a glass bubble in Arizona. There were a few reasons why the experiment failed. One was that researchers underestimated the dynamics and tension that could exist between men and women living in such close quarters "24/7/365," as they say.

Another reason the experiment failed is that they could not regulate the oxygen properly. The designers had planned that the trees they planted would be a major component of the oxygen system. But the trees died. The reason they died was that they did not put down deep roots. In nature, trees face challenges from winds and other elements. This causes them to put down roots to solidify their standing. In the Biosphere, no such challenges were present, so the trees had no motivation to root deeply. When your marriage faces storms, it can and should be an incentive to you and your spouse to deepen your commitment to each other and to your marriage. Each weathered storm makes the next one that much easier, or should I say, less difficult to face.

Marriage is and should be a serious matter. People should neither begin nor end their marriage without careful forethought. Unfortunately, we as a society have made marriage too easy to get into and far too easy to get out of. Though it is also so much more, marriage is a form of contract between two consenting adults. Can you name any other contract which either party can unilaterally end without incurring penalties?

So, let me challenge you to focus on your marriage in the coming weeks, months, and years. Determine now that you are going to do your part to make it successful and healthy. Don't worry about what your mate will or won't do. Just subtly leave this book in a conspicuous place in the house and hope they come to the same conclusion that you have. Or, be brave and let your spouse know you are committed to him or her and to doing your part to increase the harmony and intimacy in the relationship.

Many of you can do this on your own. Buy the book *10 Great Dates to Energize Your Marriage* by Dave and Claudia

Arp and just do what it says. Others of you will need more personal help in one form or another. There's no shame in that. If your tooth hurts, you are very willing to go to a dentist. So if your marriage is hurting, then there should be nothing keeping you from going to a counselor or relationship coach to get things to a better state. The investment will be minuscule in comparison to the payoff.

CHAPTER CHALLENGE

Look for an opportunity this week to thank your mate for putting up with you and assure him or her that you plan to be with them for the long haul. Also, as I suggested with the marriage ground rules, find your wedding vows and have someone write them out in calligraphy suitable for framing. Surprise your mate by hanging them in your house and let them serve as a daily reminder of your commitment to each other.

DR. SCOTT STANLEY

If you've been paying attention you know I am deeply impacted by the folks at PREP Inc. What a privilege I had to interview Dr. Scott Stanley and ask him to share a few thoughts with us about commitment.

ProductiveOutcomes.com/ dr-scott-stanley

You have to actually believe in your capacity to change for habits to permanently change.

—Charles Duhigg

CHAPTER C1
Successful Marriage
Could be Habit Forming

I OCCASIONALLY FACILITATE THE SEVEN Habits of Highly Effective People course at my local community college. This is an excellent program, and I cannot recommend it highly enough.

I once facilitated The Seven Habits for Highly Effective Families, and there is a book titled *The Seven Habits of Highly Effective Marriage*. While I am not personally familiar with the latter, I have reason to believe it contains helpful information to strengthen marriage. I base this assumption on my familiarity with the other Seven Habits programs and the value they hold for successful living. I want to share with you a listing of some of the lesser-known aspects of the Highly Effective People course, as I believe they hold application for marriage as well.

Anyone familiar with the Seven Habits knows that Habits one–three deal with individual growth and development, while Habits four–six concern our relationships with others. Habit Four—Think Win-Win—is obviously applicable to marriage. Once you decide to unite your life with someone in marriage, you give up your right to have all matters solely determined by your preferences and desires. In a successful marriage, each partner must have input into the final decisions, or the relationship will be out of balance.

Habit Five—Seek First to Understand, Then to be Understood—is one which, if truly put into practice, could put marriage professionals out of business. So often, couples get into trouble because they don't understand each other. A major reason they don't understand each other is that they are each more concerned with being understood than in understanding the other.

The Sixth Habit is Synergize, wherein parties combine their efforts and contributions so that the end result is greater than the sum of the parts they each put in. What's that old expression? "It's amazing what can be accomplished if it doesn't matter who gets the credit." I believe that certainly applies to marriage and helps to explain why Synergizing is a good habit to form.

Along with the major habits, the Seven Habits course covers a wide range of information that helps to reinforce the learning and application of the material.

One such tidbit is Dr. Covey's admonition to "Be a light, not a judge." Be honest and consider how much you appreciate being judged by anyone, let alone by your spouse. I seriously doubt you appreciate being judged, so I totally agree with the suggestion that you should focus more on looking for the good in your mate than on the bad. Strive to be a light, an encourager, a fan of your spouse and see if he or she doesn't respond in a positive manner. It might not happen overnight but likely will in the long run.

Another bit of wisdom I picked up from Dr. Covey is that "making small trim tab adjustments can yield big results." Often, we look at problems in a marriage as being so large and complicated that no remedy seems possible. What might happen if you broke that challenge into smaller, more manageable pieces? You could find that success breeds success and that over time major changes will have resulted from several smaller ones. Of course, for that to happen, you need a healthy dose of patience, which is indeed a virtue I have heard much about yet too often fail to practice. I love the expression: "God give me patience—and I mean right now!" A friend reminded me that God will not give you patience, but He will allow you to experience situations which will produce patience. Marriage is often one such situation so be grateful for the built-in training ground you have.

Another component of the Seven Habits course is "Carry your own weather." Dr. Covey uses this principle to teach the folly of expecting someone else to be responsible for your mood or your happiness. Once you delegate that responsibility outside of yourself, you are in serious trouble. You and you alone are responsible for your moods, your actions, your attitudes, etc. Of course, others can and do influence you, but to make someone else responsible is foolhardy and wrong.

I propose that marriages would improve if each partner took the challenge to master their own ups and downs rather than blaming their spouse for them. As that ability grew, each spouse could more easily choose to be in an up mood and could look forward to more enjoyable interactions within the home.

Although there are many other gems I could detail, I'll close with just one more. "You can't talk yourself out of a problem you behaved yourself into." You likely have found this out on your own, but I thought I would just remind you. So many times we mess up, hurt our spouse, and seek instant and complete forgiveness simply by saying "I'm sorry." Well, maybe it works some of the time, but depending on the depth of pain you caused, you may have to do a lot more than just offer a verbal apology. You will likely have to demonstrate your regret for having caused the pain and give your mate reason to believe it is not likely going to happen again.

CHAPTER CHALLENGE

Take stock of your marriage and look for behaviors and activities you and your spouse do out of habit rather than forethought and desire. Discuss and decide which of these habits you might want to replace with healthier, more effective habits that serve to deepen your commitment to each other and to your marriage.

*To live above
with those
we love, oh,
how that will
be glory.*

*To live below
with those we
know, now that's
another story.*
    —Source Unknown

CHAPTER C2
Marital Intelligence?
How Would You Score?

I REMEMBER AS A CHILD often hearing a radio announcer say, "The following is a test of the emergency broadcast system." A long beep would sound, after which the announcer would assure listeners that "this was only a test." He went on to say that if it had been an actual emergency, he would have given details on where to go and what to do. Again he assured, "this was only a test."

Chances are pretty good they still do that sort of testing, but since I don't often listen to the radio, I wouldn't know.

I said all that to prepare you for a test of your "Emergency Marital Preparedness System." Okay, so I just made that up, but when is the last time you and your spouse did an assessment on the state of your marriage?

When did you last ask yourselves, "Are we having enough fun time just for the two of us? Are we a team when it comes to how we handle our finances? Is our level of physical intimacy acceptable and satisfactory to both of us? Have we fallen into any ruts from which we should break out? Are we together in our faith and spiritual beliefs, practicing and living by them? Are we doing all we can to nurture our marriage and maintain our commitment to each other?"

We've all long been aware of IQ, or Intelligence Quotient. There's been a lot of buzz in recent years about EQ, or Emotional Quotient. This is a measurement of how well an individual manages him- or herself and how well he or she gets along with others. I've heard of SQ, Spiritual Quotient, or how well established a person is in the spiritual component of their life.

Well, maybe we should have MQ, which you can probably guess would be Marriage Quotient. We could develop a measurement of how well an individual is doing in his or her marriage.

While the term MQ might be new, the assessment tool is not. One of which I am familiar is Prepare-Enrich. This is an instrument which has been around for decades in one form or another. Currently, there is an online version wherein each person answers upwards of 200 questions about their marriage. The computer then combines their scores and prints out a snapshot of where they are in relationship with each other.

Among the components measured are communication and conflict resolution. Most hurting couples score fairly low in these scales. Other areas addressed include Partner Style and Habits, Friends and Family, Finances, Household Chores, etc. There are ten items measured and typically folks will score higher in some than in others.

Those areas with low scores are called Growth Areas. Slightly higher scores are described as Possible Growth Areas. Scores above 50% are called Possible Strengths and higher scores are listed as Strengths. These ten scores are then averaged together in a way that correlates to one of four categories: Vitalized, Harmonious, Conventional, and Conflicted.

According to the creators of Prepare-Enrich, Vitalized couples "are typically most satisfied with their relationship, skilled in communication and conflict resolution." Harmonious couples "also enjoy high levels of satisfaction across most areas of their relationship."

Conventional couples, which may include the majority of us, "are often committed to one another, but not as skilled in communication or conflict resolution." The one you don't want to be is Conflicted, described as having "a lower level of satisfaction and often struggle with many areas of their relationship." Unfortunately, this seems to be a rather large group in our society today.

The very good news is that MQ can be increased. For a long time IQ was thought to be fairly static. If that were true, my score of 346 would be what I am stuck with for the rest of my life (if you believe that score, I have a bridge I would like to sell you). Actually, one's IQ, EQ, SQ, and MQ can all be increased if the person takes the time and makes the effort to learn how to do life better. All marriages will

experience periods of highs and lows. Enjoy the highs—
the legal ones, that is—and be so very careful during the
lows that you don't say or do anything that might make the
situation worse and longer-lasting.

Divorce does indeed solve some problems, but it can
also create more problems than it solves. I saw a study once
that said that of couples who divorce, approximately 50%
report being happier five years later. Of those couples who
considered getting a divorce but didn't, approximately 80%
reported being happier five years later. So if you're looking
for happiness in life, the odds are more in your favor if you
stay and work on your marriage rather than breaking it off
and seeking happiness elsewhere.

A discouraging fact is that often you are a major reason
your marriage isn't working in the first place. So if you end
your marriage and start another, you are very likely going
to bring that one to ruin as well. Doesn't it make sense to
see what you might learn, to be a better spouse for the one
you have now?

If your car starts acting funny, do you automatically
replace it with a new one? Some people actually do, but
while that may be okay for a vehicle, it is not wise with a
marital partner. There are likely several people in your
area who practice marriage counseling and/or marriage
coaching. There is a difference.

For now, let me encourage you to examine your MQ, or
Marital Intelligence Quotient, and see if it might be in need
of improvement. There truly is help and hope for most every marriage to move from Conflicted to Conventional to
Harmonious and ultimately to Vitalized. Why not find out
for yourself?

CHAPTER CHALLENGE

Visit prepare-enrich.com and seek out a trained facilitator in your area. Invest the $35 to take the inventory and get an objective assessment of how you are doing in your marriage. Even more importantly, look for areas of improvement and commit to each other that you will grow in those areas.

People tend to criticize their spouse most loudly in the area where they themselves have the deepest emotional need.

—Dr. Gary Chapman

SECTION EIGHT
PLAY NICE

Emotional Needs
Must Not Be Underestimated:
We really do need each other.

I DON'T KNOW YOU PERSONALLY, but I do know something about you. Don't worry—your secret is safe with me. I know that you are a needy person. Again, don't worry that I'll blow your cover, but I do have to tell you that you are in very good company. All of us are needy and have been since the day we were born.

Part of our condition deals with our basic needs for food, clothing, and shelter, but I want to address the relationship and emotional needs that we all have. I saw a list somewhere that detailed more than 300 specific emotional needs of human beings. I prefer the shorter list of 30 that I read recently and, even better, the list of 10 that I will share with you in this chapter.

My information for this list comes from David and Teresa Ferguson, co-founders of Intimate Life Ministries in Austin, Texas. David and Teresa married at the ripe old age of 16. The morning after the wedding, a friend came by the motel and asked David if he'd like to go play pool. Since Teresa was sleeping, he figured he would go, leaving Teresa to wake up husband-less on the first day of her wedded life.

I hope your marriage started later in life and got off to a far less rocky beginning. David and Teresa have now been married more than 50 years and have helped thousands of couples around the world to develop close, intimate marriages. In one of their workshops, called More than Married, the Fergusons have participants look at ten specific relational needs that were supposed to have been met during childhood.

The needs are (in alphabetical order): acceptance, affection, appreciation, approval, attention, comfort, encouragement, respect, security, and support. These needs are ingrained into our humanity and, again, are supposed to be met by parents, siblings, extended family, etc. The problem for so many of us is that they weren't. At least they weren't met as they should have been.

During one particular exercise in the workshop, couples are asked to review the ten needs and determine if Mom or

Dad met them well. If Mom met them, participants draw a semi-circle beside the need. If Dad met them, they draw another semi-circle by the need. Thus if both met the need, there is a complete circle. If one or the other met it, there would be one half-circle, and if neither met the need, there would be no marks at all.

It grieves me to tell you that a great percentage of participants have very few whole circles. Many have half circles and far too many have no marks beside the needs. There is bad news/good news in what I'm saying here. The bad news is that we cannot undo past damage and neglect. Though we might always yearn for the comforting embrace of a mother or the encouraging words of a father, that simply may never happen. (Please don't be too hard on your parents. Chances are pretty high that they didn't get those needs met by their parents, either.)

The good news is that marriage provides an opportunity for what author Jon Acuff calls a do-over. Needs that were not satisfied in childhood and growing-up years can be met within the confines of marriage. The problem is we don't often tell our spouse what we need from them. Often we don't even know ourselves what we desire. The Fergusons developed a questionnaire to help people determine their top three relational needs. While we all have all ten, it is quite likely that some will be more impactful and needed than others. Armed with this vital information, each spouse then has a far greater chance of hitting the mark and satisfying each other's deepest needs.

Do that effectively, and you are well on your way to having a close, intimate marriage.

CHAPTER CHALLENGE

Visit greatcommandment.net, scroll down on the home page, and click on the Relational Needs Assessment, which you will find located under Free Resources. Set aside 30–60 minutes to go over the assessment individually and to discuss your results together. Your challenge then is to look for ways in the coming days, weeks, and years to satisfy your mate's needs.

*If you are
depressed,
you are living
in the past.*

*If you are
anxious, you
are living in
the future.*

*If you are at
peace, you
are living in
the present.*

  —Lao Tzu

CHAPTER E1
Yesterday is Gone—Isn't It?

FRANKLIN **D.** **R**OOSEVELT RIGHTLY proclaimed that December 7 would forever be a day of infamy for us as a nation. November 3 is such a day for me, as that is the day my mother died. You never got to meet Sylvia Price. From what I hear, you would have liked her. She was said to be a devoted wife and mother, and she apparently took an active role in supporting the PTA and other of her children's events.

My memories from those early years are woefully lacking. I do remember making trips from our home in Providence, Rhode Island, to Mass General Hospital in Boston, or to Miriam Hospital, which was located directly across the street from my elementary school.

Wow, it just dawned on me that I must have spent many moments at recess knowing my mother was being held captive and detached from me just literally feet away, yet not fully comprehending the reason why. Here I am 66 years old, and that thought still brings tears to my eyes for the young boy who so needed and missed his mother. Give me just a moment, please.

Okay, I'm back, but I actually did take a few days to come back to this chapter. That memory hit me like a proverbial ton of bricks. It came with no warning and disabled me from continuing with my task. I wrote in *PLAY NICE in Your Sandbox at Work* about this also occurring when I took my wife to see the movie *Stepmom* starring Julia Roberts, Ed Harris, and Susan Sarandon. It is a very moving story about a young mother who is dying of cancer and about to leave her two young children, who, by the way, just so happened to be about the same age as my older brother and I were when our mom died of cancer. The only part of my story missing in the movie is that my younger sister was not in it.

I had two separate breakdowns during that movie, each lasting approximately ten minutes. During the first, I was clueless as to what was occurring. I just had this overwhelming sense of sadness and grief. In the second outburst, the reason became crystal clear. I realized that while everyone else in the theater was watching Susan Sarandon die of cancer, I was watching my own mother figuratively die right before my eyes. At that moment, while I was in my late 40's physically, emotionally I was an eight-year-old grieving the loss of my mother.

I make no apology for my outbursts and certainly feel no shame. The point I hope to drive home in this chapter is that your spouse has hurtful experiences from his or her past, memories of which can arise out of nowhere and with a ferociousness for which they will likely not be prepared. It is precisely at these moments when you, more than any other of the billions of us on the planet, can be a source of comfort, care, and healing.

When your spouse is recalling a memory of a traumatic and hurtful experience, he or she is likely not going to be very pleasant, loving, or easy to be around. He or she may snap at you, yell at you, throw a fit, or have any number of reactions comparable to those of a hurt, young child. They are not doing this on purpose, but ideally, you can purposely choose how to respond. If you choose to join them in any form of negative emotion, you might want to cancel any plans you may have had for a joyful time together, for that's not likely going to happen.

If, on the other hand, you can somehow choose to minister to his or her pain with soft, comforting words, a gentle hug, or anything else a young child might appreciate, your chances of responding appropriately are significantly increased. Please don't talk down to your spouse as if he or she really is a child—they are not. It's just that at that particular moment, they are hurting, and they need your comforting.

Oh, that more couples would be aware that the painful experiences of their past have a dramatic and powerful impact on their relationships today. Men, the chances are pretty high that you pay the price at times for other men who have hurt your wife in the past. That is certainly not fair, but neither is it purposeful or mean-spirited. It's more likely that you just said or did something that she connected with an earlier memory. Wives, please note the same about your husbands. He does not mean to lash out at you at those times, but if you have just somehow reminded him—consciously or unconsciously—of a hurtful moment in his past, he will quite likely take it out on you.

These can be moments of immense healing and growth, but only if you handle them well. Fortunately, marriage provides numerous opportunities for practice. I encourage you, in those moments, to purposely choose to be extra gentle, loving and sweet to your mate. They need you and you need them, and together you really can have a wonderful marriage.

CHAPTER CHALLENGE

Take some time to consider the wounds from your past and determine if they may be the cause of distress in your life and/or your marriage. If so, please don't settle or feel you are stuck in that condition. Invest some time, money, and effort into counseling or coaching to learn how to put these memories in proper perspective. They will never go away entirely, but you can diminish their destructive impact.

BILL & PAM FARREL

In this next interview marriage experts Bill & Pam Farrel share several key points, including how past hurts impact their present-day marriage.

**ProductiveOutcomes.com/
bill-pam-farrel**

BONUS:

Bill and Pam created a special video to be included in this book. I invite you to spend a few minutes learning about their year-long argument, and how they eventually resolved it.

staging.love-wise.com/sandbox

*And you will
know the truth,
and the truth
will set you free!*

—**John 8:32**

CHAPTER **E2**
Hidden Issues:
What you don't know can hurt you

C AN YOU REMEMBER THE delight of your first ride on a merry-go-round? I think I can vividly remember the thrill of victory when, after numerous failed attempts, I finally grabbed my first ring. Of course, I'm reaching the age where accuracy and facts have little relevance in the telling of a story.

While riding a merry-go-round can be a pleasant experience in childhood, the same cannot be said of 'round and 'round arguments, over the same issues that most couples seem to find themselves in at recurring moments in their marriage. While very common, it can also be very frustrating. If you find yourself in that situation, you might consider that the reason the argument keeps re-appearing is that you have never successfully gotten to the underlying root cause of the issue.

Researchers at the PREP marriage enrichment program, authors of *Fighting For Your Marriage,* and *A Lasting Promise,* have concluded that there is a distinction between events and issues, and they further differentiate between known issues and those about which we are unaware.[4] They refer to this latter category as "hidden issues." If hidden issues are the reason for your frequent and repeated arguments, you just might want to discover what they are if you have any hope of finally putting them to rest.

Events are occurrences which can cause distress and disharmony. Events appear as an unexpected bill, a forgotten appointment, illness, or any number of other examples we could use.

Issues are concerns each has for the marriage or about the other but which they are likely reluctant to voice for one reason or another.

Hidden issues are the deeper dynamics that underlie and often stoke the fires of discontent without ever being identified as the culprit.

Unfortunately, most couples only deal with their issues in the context of their events. In other words, they are not totally pleased with some aspect of their mate, but rather than bring it up for appropriate and productive discussion, they wait and vent when some event that presents an opportunity to unleash and unload on their partner occurs.

---

4   Markman, H. J., Stanley, S. M., & Blumberg, S. L. (2010). Fighting for your marriage. San Francisco: Jossey-Bass.

Stanley, S., Trathen, D., McCain, S., & Bryan, M. (2014). A lasting promise: The Christian Guide to Fighting for Your Marriage. San Francisco: Jossey Bass, Inc.

Dealing with issues only in the context of events will just about always lead to a disappointing outcome. Such behavior puts each in a reactive rather than a proactive mode. The former is a prescription for escalation and negativity, while the latter could lead to resolution and restored happiness.

The folks at PREP recommend you handle events together as they arise because, by definition, you cannot predict them in advance. They also recommend you schedule regular times when you can sit down and calmly discuss any relationship issues which have arisen between you. This, they suggest, will help you to keep small matters small rather than letting them fester and grow to unmanageable dimensions.

Hidden issues pose a much more serious threat to a marriage. They are described as being "unexpressed expectations, needs, and concerns that can cause great damage in a marriage." Hidden issues are often the real issue in many disputes, but they are kind of like the proverbial "elephant in the living room" that we try to ignore.

Hidden issues, if left in the dark, will often undermine a couple's ability to draw close together on an intimate level. While hidden issues are a common experience in most all marriages, they are typically there for a reason. One or both may consider them to be too threatening to bring up directly, so they are kept hidden from the other, or each may be truly unaware of their existence.

Some signs that a hidden issue may be at the root of a marital dispute:

- Spinning your wheels and seemingly going around and around but not getting anywhere constructive.

- Avoidance of certain topics, which are considered too dangerous to discuss.

- Trivial triggers where relatively small incidents can generate a major reaction.

- Score keeping when one or both feel they are contributing more than they are receiving from the relationship.

Again, if these sound familiar to you, please know you are by no means alone. They do not at all indicate you married the wrong person or that your marriage is doomed. Such repetitive behaviors are a pretty good indication, however, that remedial intervention is necessary, because they are not likely to go away or improve without being addressed.

So what exactly are these "hidden issues?" I am so glad you asked. What follows is a list of the common ones, but please note you may have others which did not make the list but which can be just as destructive.

One very common hidden issue is "Power and Control," where each may wonder who gets to make the important decisions in the relationship. Some may feel their needs are not given as much importance as their mate's and resent the inequality. If so, there could be an underlying issue of power and control, which will impact the couple in typically negative and frustrating ways.

A second common hidden issue is "Caring," when one or both begin to question just how much his or her spouse really cares about him or her. When this hidden issue is present, each may wonder if the other's love is unconditional or solely based on a certain level of performance.

Another very common hidden issue in many marriages is "Recognition," where one or both begin to wonder if his or her partner sees the efforts and contributions they make in the marriage. While "Caring" issues involve concerns of being cared for or loved, "Recognition" issues are about whether or not you feel valued by your spouse for who you are and what you contribute to the marriage.

"Commitment" is another common hidden issue in many marriages. Here the focus is on the long-term view of the relationship. Many spouses will hold back from fully investing in the marriage if they feel the other may not reciprocate or if they are perhaps not in it for the long haul.

The fifth hidden issue cited in the PREP program is "Integrity." This issue occurs when one feels challenged for who they see themselves to be. Consider for a moment whether you have ever gotten seriously upset when your spouse questioned your intent or motives. Is it possible that your reaction was worse than the presenting offense? That is likely because you felt your integrity was being questioned and you quickly grew defensive.

And, lastly, "Acceptance," which is thought to be a key concern for most of us. We all have some degree of fear of rejection and wonder at times whether others accept us for who we are. While in most relationships this is not a major concern, it can absolutely be a threat in marriage.

So there you have it: a suggested list of reasons why you and your spouse have recurring arguments or disagreements that seemingly never get resolved. They go away for a while, only to return with predictability and, often, increasing intensity. But take heart. With time and effort you can uncover and successfully address any hidden issues which may be present in your marriage. The LUV Talk, which you read about in Chapter Y2, is a wonderful tool to help you get to the bottom of your difficulties and then to strategize how to overcome them.

In the meantime, I'll leave you with some thoughts by a couple of experts in the field. Dr. Alan Godwin wrote *How to Solve Your People Problems: Dealing with your difficult relationships*. In his book, he makes the point that far too often couples attempt to solve problems before they truly understand the core issues underlying the problem. This is akin, he says, to putting a band-aid on skin cancer. You might help the issue seem to go away temporarily, but it is bound to reappear down the road.

Dr. Susan Heitler is a practicing psychologist in Denver. In her book *The Power of Two: Secrets to a Strong & Loving Marriage*, she writes "Solution-building is often surprisingly easy. After two initially antagonistic parties have cooperatively explored their underlying concerns, they most often discover that their apparent conflict involved concerns that are complementary. One creative solution can make everyone happy."

CHAPTER CHALLENGE

Schedule a time to discuss the list
of Hidden Issues and determine
which, if any, may be occurring
in your marriage. If necessary,
choose a professional counselor
or coach who can help you get the
answers you seek. I know I make
that recommendation frequently
in this book, and I know counseling
can get expensive after a while. I
assure you, however, it is far less
costly than divorce—and I don't just
mean monetarily.

CLINT AND PENNY BRAGG

So many couples give up any hope that they can ever succeed as a couple. You're about to hear from a couple who did call it quits on their marriage, but reconnected several years later and are still going strong today.

**ProductiveOutcomes.com/
clint-penny-bragg**

Many marriages would be better if the husband and the wife clearly understood that they are on the same side.

—**Zig Ziglar**

CLOSING
THOUGHTS
Keep the Love Alive:
Random Tips for Healthy Marriage

I T'S BEEN QUITE THE journey and experience to write this book. While I do believe it contains valuable and helpful information, I realize no one book can contain all the wisdom, knowledge, and information necessary to completely address marital and family wellness. There was so much more I wanted to include, but which didn't quite seem to fit. So I decided to put some of that information here in what you might call a hodgepodge chapter.

A) Most marriages start off with high hopes that their love will always remain exactly as it is in the beginning. I hate to be the one to tell you, but that is just not possible. In this interview Jay and Laura Laffoon talk about specific ways to keep the spark alive throughout your marriage.

**ProductiveOutcomes.com/
jay-laura-laffoon**

B) Dr. Gary Chapman has likely impacted more people's marriages than any other individual on the planet. His book *The Five Love Languages* helps couples to put their good intentions to positive application. You would do well to get your own copy of the book to see how you and your spouse can take your love for each other to a deeper level. You can also visit fivelovelanguages.com and take a short survey to see what your and your mate's particular language might be. Once identified, you should have a better shot at speaking it.

C) I appreciate the advice given in *Fighting For Your Marriage* that couples should designate two nights per week to focus on their marriage. One should be a fun night, and the other should be an issues night. You need to protect these two nights from distraction and focus on their specific purpose.

D) Bill and Pam Farrel are the authors of *Men are like Waffles, Women are like Spaghetti* and several other books. Among their numerous tips for healthy marriage are that a couple should pay special attention to their relationship two times each day. The first is when they part from each other at the beginning of the day, and the second, you may have guessed, is when they reunite. I absolutely agree that you should not leave your spouse for the day without somehow reminding him or her that he or she is the most important person in your life.

A great habit to form at the end of the work day is to embrace and engage in a ten-second kiss. When you connect up after being apart from each other, you are at different places physically, mentally, emotionally, etc. A ten-second embrace and kiss serve to connect you in ways that will likely surprise you, and which will bode well for an enjoyable evening together.

E) A common threat to marriage is routine and stagnation but, as you have read in this book, this need not be the case for you and your marriage. Here's another tip I picked up somewhere, but cannot remember where or from whom. Each day ask your mate, "What can I do to make your day better?" By sincerely asking this question, you are reminding your mate of how much you value and appreciate him or her. Word to the wise: Listen carefully to the answer and be sure to follow through. Failure to do so is far worse than not asking the question in the first place.

F) I do know the source for this next tip, as it is one my wife and I discovered for ourselves several years ago. I talk for a living. All day long, I'm mediating, marriage coaching, giving workshops, etc. When I come home, the last thing I want to do is talk. My wife is a quiet person. She's extremely personable, and people are drawn to her, but she doesn't talk all that much during her day. When she comes home, what's the first thing she wants to do? Talk. Do you see a problem here? And a problem it was for quite a while as I would be trying to unwind from a day of engaging with other people and she would want (deservedly so) to engage with me.

We finally agreed that when I came home, we would engage in a ten-second kiss and restate our love for each other, but then I was allowed to have 15–30 minutes of downtime. A time when I didn't have to talk on the phone or do anything other than veg out. After that time, however, I was to be in full connection mode, and we could discuss our days or anything else that came up. This has worked remarkably well over the years, and I offer it to you as something to consider.

G) It often seems that no one stays married these days. While it is true that many marriages end in divorce, I'm happy to tell you that many couples do stay together until parted by death. You just don't hear about them as often as you do the ones who decide to call it quits. I think it is important to celebrate milestones in your marriage. Yearly anniversaries are worth acknowledging in some fashion. Your 25th and 50th should certainly be highlighted, but you can find other times to celebrate more frequently.

Here's one way to build in extra milestones. Check out therobertd.com where you'll find a quick and easy way to calculate how many days you have been married, how many days you or your children have been alive, etc.

The question of how many days we had been married came to my mind while out to dinner with my wife some years ago. I checked and joyfully learned that that very day was our 10,000th day of marriage. That was pretty cool, but the story doesn't end there. A few weeks later, I happened to be visiting with a couple who got married the week before we did and shared that story. They checked and realized that on their 10,000th day of marriage, they were at their daughter's graduation from a small Christian college where she received a certificate for being the 10,000th graduate from that college. You may choose to believe this was all just grand coincidence. I don't have enough faith to accept that, so please forgive me if I choose to believe it was Divine Intervention.

H) We've all heard some pretty ridiculous expressions in our lifetimes. One of my nominees for an award winner is "Sticks and stones may break my bones, but words will never hurt me." It's a pretty safe bet that you have discovered that's just not true.

Another nominee is from a Stephen Stills song, "Love the One You're With," which suggests it is perfectly fine to be intimate with anyone you choose whenever your spouse is not nearby. Just ask anyone who has endured the painful ramifications of such a decision, and I think you'll agree that advice is just dead wrong.

Willard Harley, the author of *His Needs, Her Needs*, refers to adultery as being the single worst thing one person can do to another. With that said, I've heard that 80% of couples who endure affairs do not divorce. You might be as surprised as I was to hear that, but the statistics don't lie. Most couples can overcome infidelity and build a stronger marriage as a result.

Anne Bercht wrote a book with the strangest title I've ever heard. It's called *My Husband's Affair Became the Best Thing That Ever Happened to Me*. Ann and her husband Brian, the "cheater," lead an organization called the Beyond Affairs Network (beyondaffairs.com), through which they help couples overcome this horrific attack on their marriage.

The odds are that you know a couple who is in the midst of dealing with this as we speak—or write. Please don't be silent. If you know a couple who is struggling in their marriage, be brave and let them know help is available. You and they might be so glad you did.

And, finally…

I) You may have noticed that I am a fan of quotes that help to bring life into perspective. I read a quote by George Eliot that said, "What do we live for if it is not to make life less difficult for each other?" I was impressed with the quote and searched for more information about Mr. Eliot. I was surprised to learn that George Eliot was actually the pen name for Mary Ann Evans, a 19th-century author of several books—*Silas Marner* being the only one I recognize. I think I was supposed to read it in high school, but that was last century, so we'll just move on.

From what I gather, this quote did not directly relate to marriage, but it sure does seem to have great application there. What would our marriages be like if each spouse adopted the mindset that his or her primary purpose in the union was to make life less difficult for the other?

Here's another of her quotes that also seems fitting for marriage. Just substitute the word "spouse" for "friend" and I think you'll agree. She wrote, "A friend is one to whom one may pour out the contents of one's heart, chaff and grain together, knowing that gentle hands will take and sift it, keep what is worth keeping, and with a breath of kindness, blow the rest away."

In my search, I also found two humorous quotes of hers I just have to share with you: "And, of course, men know best about everything, except what women know better." And "Blessed is the man who, having nothing to say, abstains from giving us wordy evidence of the fact."

The final George Eliot quote that got my attention is directly related to marriage—or at least should be. She wrote: "What greater thing is there for two human souls, than to feel that they are joined for life—to strengthen each other in all labor, to rest on each other in all sorrow, to minister to each other in all pain, to be one with each other in silent unspeakable memories at the moment of the last parting?"

Oh, that couples had such a mindset before and during their marriage. Those who make their living off divorce may not approve, but I think our society would surely benefit.

EPILOGUE

I GUESS I'M NAÏVE IN a lot of areas, but I learned a new word from reading Dear Abby. I'm not her biggest fan, but I do like to see what advice she gives to people, especially in the area of marriage and relationships. The new word to which I refer is "polyamory." I had a pretty good idea of what it meant, but a little research confirmed for me that polyamory means "many loves." Apparently, it's a lifestyle wherein people are free to love and be loved by anyone or anyones, or perhaps anything of their choosing. One website I checked admitted that this is not a lifestyle for everyone and not even for the majority. They claim that

95% of cohabitating couples expect monogamous behavior from their partner and that the percentage for married couples is "a few points higher."

This Dear Abby article brought to my mind an editorial I read in my local newspaper, in which the writer cautioned advocates of gay marriage to be careful what they asked for because being married could make them just as miserable as the rest of us—or something to that effect.

I don't know about you, but I'm getting awfully tired of the seemingly endless attacks on marriage that fill our media these days. Yes, I realize we still live in America, and yes, I know it is each person's right to live their lives as they choose just as long as they "don't hurt anyone." But therein lies the problem. Attacks on marriage and the resultant downward trend of marriage is hurting all of us—especially the youngest and most vulnerable of our population.

I will certainly admit that marriage is not a perfect institution. I will also admit that we as a society have done a horrible job of preserving and protecting marriage. But the research is clear that healthy marriage provides a genuine benefit to individuals and to our nation. The Institute for American Values is "a non-partisan organization dedicated to strengthening families and civil society in the US and the world." This organization regularly brings together scholars from various fields of study. I know that some of these researchers claim a Christian faith. Others I know to be Jewish, and others I believe claim no religious faith at all. I only mention that because many have made the argument that marriage is just a matter of religion and that simply is not the case.

These scholars frequently issue results of their findings in various journals and publications. One such publication is "Why Marriage Matters, Second Edition: Twenty-six

Conclusions from the Social Sciences." This booklet is 43 pages long, including ten pages of research footnotes. Here are their three fundamental conclusions:

- Marriage is an important social good;
- Marriage is an important public good; and
- The benefits of marriage extend to poor and minority communities.

They also concluded that "whether American society and, indeed, the world, succeeds or fails in building a healthy marriage culture is clearly a matter of legitimate public concern. In particular, marriage is an issue of paramount importance if we wish to help the most vulnerable members of our society: the poor, minorities and children."

By almost any standard of measurement, children do better in homes with two happily married parents than they do in homes with single or cohabitating parents. There truly is a difference. It is certainly true that many children from "broken" homes do quite well in life. And, as Archie Bunker once said, "The reverse vice is also true" that many children from intact two-parent homes make poor decisions and get into trouble. The odds, however, speak clearly that it is in the best interest of children to grow up with a mother and father who love them and each other.

On a more personal note, I am firm in my belief that we are designed for, and crave, intimacy in our lives. We each have a deep-seated desire to be understood, to be valued and appreciated, especially by one person. It is virtually impossible to be intimately connected with numerous people at the same time. I've heard intimacy defined as being "into-me-see," and that just doesn't work with everyone you know or meet.

The appeal of multiple romances fades dramatically when one considers the consequences of STDs, heartbreak, jealousy, etc. We've also bought into the lie that sex equals love. Go to any supermarket checkout line and see the headlines about how to have better sex and on and on ad nauseum. Trust me, I'm not against sex, but it is love and connection that we truly seek and that requires a monogamous, committed relationship.

I am confident in my assertion that there is nothing wrong with the concept of marriage. There is plenty wrong with the fact that many people get into marriage without having a clue what they are doing and that many end their marriage when help and healing are readily available. There is also plenty wrong with attacking marriage, for as my friend New Mexico State Senator Bill Sharer puts it, "Marriage is the first and most basic organization of civilization—it is the first and best child-welfare system. Strong marriage builds strong families, strong families build strong societies, strong societies build strong relationships, and strong relationships build peace." Therefore, he concludes, "Marriage = Peace."

While it may not be a popular opinion, the research is clear that traditional marriage is the healthiest lifestyle and that faithfulness within marriage is absolutely the best way to live. Treat your marriage poorly, and you'll likely suffer deep and long lasting consequences. Treat your marriage well, and you and the rest of us will likely reap great rewards. And, as I mentioned, resources to help folks prepare for marriage and to repair one when necessary abound in our culture.

I've long been a fan of Yogi Berra and of his ability to turn the English language upside down. One of my favorite

"Berra-isms" is, "Oh nobody ever goes to that restaurant anymore—it's always too crowded." He is also alleged to have said that "baseball is 90% mental and the other half is physical." Permit me, if you will, to say that life is 90% relational, and I'm not quite sure what the other half is.

I have also appreciated a quote attributed to David Matthews: "All fundamental problems are at their core problems of relationships. It follows then that all real solutions consist of reordering relationships." It is my hope that this book has encouraged you to view your marriage and family in a proper perspective and helped to equip you to make your relationship as healthy as possible.

CALL TO ACTION

I hope you enjoyed reading *PLAY NICE in Your Sandbox at Home*. If so, I'm confident you'll also enjoy the other books in the Sandbox series:

PLAY NICE in Your Sandbox at Work
While written with a work emphasis, just about all of the information you'll find there will also apply to your relationships with family members and friends. And,

PLAY NICE in Your Sandbox at Church
(Due out in the Fall of 2018)

I'd love to read your comments about how you applied concepts covered in this book or other thoughts about minimizing and/or resolving conflict. I promise to give you credit if I use your contributions in a future book or Blog post.

Send your comments, questions
or concerns to me at:
ron@PlayNiceInYourSandbox.com

About the Author

RON PRICE, MA, OWNS and operates Productive Outcomes, Inc. where he provides mediation and arbitration, along with life and marriage coaching, workplace training, and public speaking services.

Ron's background in the field of conflict resolution started with a BA in Sociology, which he earned at the University of Rhode Island in 1974, followed by a master's degree in Counseling from the University of New Mexico in 1994.

Since 1987, he has mediated thousands of cases for the Eleventh Judicial District Court in San Juan County, New Mexico, and coached hundreds of people on how to improve their relationships since 2001.

Ron is trained by such diverse entities as the Association for Conflict Resolution, the San Diego Center for Mediation, The Better Business Bureau, the United States Postal Service, and the Association of Family and Conciliation Courts. He is an expert at figuring out not only how people tick, but how to help them tick in harmony with others.

Ron is happily married to Maridell Price, with whom he has been sharing a heart and a home since December 28, 1980. They have no children, but at present one dog and way too many cats. (Hint: one of them is a cat lover, and the other one loves her.)

RESOURCES

COUPLES MAY FAIL IN their marriage, but none can say it was because help was not available. As I've written throughout this book there is an abundance of resources to help address any and all challenges couples may face in their marriage. Along with those I cited in the book, here, in no particular order are a few of my other favorites. I am aware of many more. Feel free to contact me to address a specific situation you or someone you know is facing.

AUTHORS/BOOKS:

10 Great Dates series
by Dave and Claudia Arp

Fight Your Way to a Better Marriage
by Dr. Greg Smalley

He Said She Said
by Jay and Laura Laffoon

Can You Hear Me Now?
by Dr. Dallas Demmitt and Nancy Demmitt

How We Love
by Milan and Kay Yerkovich

The Vow
by Kim and Krickitt Carpenter

Boundaries
by Drs. Henry Cloud and John Townsend

Fighting for Your Marriage
by Drs. Howard Markman, Scott Stanley,
and Susan Blumberg

**A Lasting Promise:
a Christian Guide to Fighting for Your Marriage**
by Drs. Scott Stanley, Daniel Trathen,
B. Milton Bryan and Savanna McCain

How To Stay Married and Love It!
by Jim and Nancy Landrum

Change Your Brain, Change Your Life
by Dr. Daniel Amen

Switch on Your Brain
by Dr. Caroline Leaf

Laugh Your Way to a Better Marriage
by Mark Gungor

Soul Healing Love
by Drs. Tom and Beverly Rodgers

**Every Man's Battle: Every Man's Guide to Winning the
War on Sexual Temptation One Victory at a Time**
by Stephen Arterburn, Fred Stoeker, and Mike Yorkey

Turn Up the Heat
by Dr. Kevin Leman

Sheet Music
by Dr. Kevin Leman

ORGANIZATIONS OR PROGRAMS FOR:

TROUBLED MARRIAGES:

retrouvaille.org
Catholic-based

nationalmarriage.com
National Institute of Marriage

marriagedynamics.com
A New Beginning

rodgerscc.com
Rodgers Christian Counseling Center

beyondaffairsnetwork.com
Brian and Anne Bercht

divorcebusting.com
Michelle Weiner Davis

smalley.cc
Smalley Institute

richardmarksphd.com
Richard Marks

hoperestored.focusonthefamily.com
Focus on the Family

GOOD MARRIAGES
THAT COULD STAND A BOOST:

PREPinc.com
portal to all the resources offered by PREP
(Scott Stanley, Howard Markman, and colleagues)

lovetakeslearning.com
online version of PREP (called ePREP)
Love Takes Learning - PREP

familylifeministries.org/weekend-to-remember
A Weekend to Remember
Family Life Ministries

jayandlaura.com/ultimate-date-night
Ultimate Date Night
Jay and Laura Laffoon

markgungor.com
Laugh Your Way to a Better Marriage
Mark Gungor

love-wise.com
Men are like Waffles, Women are like Spaghetti
Bill and Pam Farrel

PRE-MARRIAGE:

Prepare-Enrich.com

PARENTING:

fatherhood.org

loveandlogic.com

mensfraternity.com

STEP-FAMILIES:

smartstepfamilies.com

FINANCES:

daveramsey.com
Dave Ramsey Financial Peace University

MoneyHabitudes.com
Syble Solomon

Learn more at

PlayNiceInYourSandbox.com